MAN & YOSEMITE

TITLE PAGE. T.C. Roche. *Reflection of Washington Tower, Royal Arches and North Dome. 1870.* Roche was an itinerant photographer who worked with Matthew Brady photographing the Civil War, and later was hired by the New York based firm of E. & H.T. Anthony to travel west and make stereocard views of Yosemite. [P]

AMERICAN VIEWS.

Yosemite Valley, Cal.

98.—Reflection of Washington Tower, Royal Arches and North Dome.

MAN & YOSEMITE
A PHOTOGRAPHER'S VIEW OF THE EARLY YEARS

BY TED ORLAND

THE IMAGE CONTINUUM PRESS

Published by
The Image Continuum Press
1017 Seabright Avenue
Santa Cruz CA 95062

ISBN 0-9614547-0-9 (hardcover)
ISBN 0-9614547-1-7 (softcover)
ISBN 0-9614547-2-5 (spec. ed.)

Typesetting by Kennedy Typography (Santa Cruz)
and Graham Mackintosh (Santa Barbara).
Printed in Japan by Dai Nippon,
With special thanks to Kohei Tsumori.

10 9 8 7 6 5 4 3

Foreword

My friends tell me it is perilous for a photographer to take up writing — and I agree! The highly personal belief system required of an artist is rarely compatible with the broad impartiality expected of a critic. I am equally convinced, however, that those who practice the art are in a unique position to say something important about the play of forces that shape their fellow artists' work. That belief, combined with my curiosity about the early history of Yosemite Valley, led me to think about the forces at work there in the nineteenth century, and about the role photography played in revealing — and sometimes determining — the equilibrium point that would come to exist between Man and Yosemite.

My task was made a bit easier by the simple historical fact that Yosemite Valley was not visited by white men until *after* the invention of photography, at a time when the aesthetics of American landscape photography were still just developing; as a result, photographers working there were highly visible participants in both the history of Yosemite and the history of photography. By overlaying decades of successive images taken from identical vantage points, we can follow the changing ecology of Yosemite, and often deduce the causes of such change. By viewing pictures of its early visitors, we see revealed in the clothes they wore and the activities they pursued, an evolution in public attitude about the wilderness. And by studying the photgraphs as *photographs*, we can watch the increasing technical capabilities of the medium subtly alter the artists' visual sense — and by extension *our* sense — of what constitutes the "real" Yosemite.

That last question — of knowing just what is "real" — is the trickiest to confront. A photograph may be worth a thousand words, but if so, all those words are *nouns* — the lens resolves a myriad of *objects* with startling clarity, yet remains infuriatingly silent about *events* that occurred even one second to either side of the moment the shutter was open. When writing about images, the natural temptation is to draw conclusions, to "tell a story" — the peril is that when a story-line is drawn between the discontinuous points of time captured by the film, history will be altered to fit the available pictures. The secret, I think, is to keep your eye always on the far horizon, using objects as adjectives, as ambience, to hint at the *direction* history will lead. The written word and the visual image each create their own separate reality, incomplete when taken alone, and distorted when one is reduced to simply illustrating the other. My hope is that *Man & Yosemite* will in some small way nurture the idea that words and photographs, taken together, reveal certain qualities about ourselves and our relationship to the land that are not recorded with fidelity by either craft alone.

I also hope, quite simply, that you *enjoy* this book — after all, I've certainly enjoyed working on it! Researching these early writings and images proved an inherently satisfying task, one to which I happily committed my free time over a span of several years. This leisurely pace yielded its own reward, allowing time for my understanding of Yosemite to evolve and mature, time to work with the text until I felt truly comfortable with even its most subjective judgements.

In the course of my research, the only real problem I encountered lay in getting useable reproduction prints of the material I located. One prestigious museum, in response to my purchase order for 4 × 5 copy negatives of Muybridge Mammoth Plates, sent 35mm snapshots of *halftone reproductions* pictured in one of their catalogs! Another equally famous research library would provide only prints of such uniformly dismal quality as to be worthless for most any purpose. Fortunately, there exist multiple copies of even relatively rare Yosemite images, and eventually I located a handful of wonderfully helpful people through whom I was able to obtain access to most all the material I needed.

Primary among these sources has been Jack Gyer, long-term Curator of the National Park Service Museum at Yosemite. Jack offered not only his personal help and encouragement, but also his permission to explore in depth the Museum Collection, and then make my own 4 × 5 copy negatives of material I found valuable. Since Jack's recent retirement, Barbara Beroza (his successor) has offered equally helpful and enthusiastic support.

Among private collectors, Virginia Adams was in many ways a catalyst to my undertaking this project in the first place. I met Virginia on my first trip to Yosemite in 1967, and each succeeding summer when I returned to the Valley, she related additional intriguing bits of information about the area from her readings and personal memories. Then, about 1971, I assisted at a workshop in Yosemite titled "Making a Photographic Book", co-taught by Ansel with photo historians Beaumont and Nancy Newhall; the workshop concentrated upon producing a mock-up of a book that would compare early historical photographs of the Valley with contemporary images made from the same vantage points by workshop students. At the time, nothing tangible materialized from the effort, but working with those early images convinced me the material was inherently interesting, and that *someone* should take up the challenge.

Later, when this project had moved along some distance, both Virginia and another collector, Richard Pitman, generously opened their personal Yosemite collections to me. Adding the copy negatives I made of their holdings to those I made of the Park Service collection in turn allowed me to aim for much higher reproduction quality in the finished book. Taking on that work myself (and then deciding to tackle the layout, typesetting, paste-up, and related tasks as well) all stemmed simply from a desire to do it *right* — an approach that soon blurred the line traditionally separating author from publisher, and placed me in the position of self-publishing this work.

That last item — self-publishing — turns out to be an art unto itself. The truth of that became evident when self-imposed deadlines for completing this book evaporated before me with monotonous regularity as I grappled with learning the successive intricacies of editing, graphic design, printing and distribution. But in retrospect the slow pace is easily outweighed by the reward — not often granted one in this age of specialization — of mastering each task to be done, and personally guiding it through to completion. I would quickly add that *Man & Yosemite* is equally imbued with the ideas of those who guided *me* along the way. Besides those friends already mentioned, I am forever indebted to Lillian Marks and the late Saul Marks, to Frances Connolly, David Bayles, Sally Mann, Boone Morrison, and to many other close friends who each played an essential role in the project. And lastly, my very special thanks to Dave Bohn for so generously sharing his time and knowledge throughout the project, from proofreading the first manuscript to helping prepare for the final press run.

TED ORLAND

PLATE 1. Ted Orland. *The Yosemite Valley.*

The Original Inhabitants

The Indians were first. Paiutes entered Yosemite somewhat more than two thousand years ago, crossing over from the drier east side of the Sierra to hunt and gather food during the summer months. A few centuries later, Miwoks from the great Central Valley of California entered from the west in greater numbers, establishing permanent village sites in Yosemite Valley. They called their home "Ahwahnee", which translates to "deep, grassy valley"; by extension this also became the name of their principal village, and eventually the name of the tribe itself. Our present name for the Valley—Yosemite—is simply a corruption of the Ahwahneechee word "Uzumati", meaning "grizzly bear".

Perhaps because the mild California climate did not offer what Toynbee would term "the challenge of adversity", the Miwok civilization did not "progress" in the traditional Western sense of the word, and left few tangible monuments to its existence—no permanent structures, no cultivated plants, no domesticated animals. But if their culture was notably unconcerned with the physical trappings of posterity, its wealth of games and crafts, myth and ritual, attest to a healthy vitality of the spirit. To ask whether such a situation was tranquil, or simply stagnant, is to judge them by our standards. They lived at peace with the Land and (generally) with their neighbors for a very considerable number of centuries, and for them that was sufficient.

That situation changed radically in the late seventeenth century with the arrival of the Spanish, who carried with them (among other things) diphtheria, smallpox, pneumonia, syphilis, and a plethora of other communicable diseases, which together exacted a predictable toll upon a race never previously exposed to European sicknesses. The Ahwahneechees were decimated by a "fatal black sickness"—probably the cholera epidemic of 1833—to the extent that Yosemite Valley was left entirely uninhabited from that date until nearly the time of first entry by white men, in 1851. That entry—by volunteer militia, in pursuit of Indians who had resisted the incursion of gold mining operations further down the Merced River—resulted in the razing of the Indians' village and, soon afterward, to their forced exodus to a reservation near Fresno. It was a familiar story, often repeated elsewhere on the frontier with only the dates and place names changed.

Our knowledge of that facet of Yosemite history derives almost entirely from a single original source, *Discovery of the Yosemite,* by Lafayette Bunnell. (Long out of print since its original publication in 1880, the book has recently reappeared in paperback). Bunnell, a member of the "Mariposa Battalion" that "discovered" Yosemite, gives a splendidly detailed account of events of that time, though heavily colored by a Victorian perspective that strained mightily to integrate its ideal of the Indian-as-Noble-Savage with the reality of its methodical extermination of that same race. Many, many statements in the book are painfully reminiscent of the words of an Air Cavalry Commander in Viet Nam who told us, "We had to destroy their village in order to save them".

The Indians pictured here are Paiutes, coming to trade in Yosemite Valley from their homes on the east side of the Sierra. It is a handsome portrait, taken at a revealing moment in time, capturing a hint of the strength and integrity of the aboriginal Indian culture—but suggesting also through their clothing an already-acquired dependence upon the white man. Probably born at about the time their tribe first encountered white men in large numbers, they will be the last of their people. The year is 1875.

Their opposites (Plate 3), prominent then but now long forgotten, number from among the first generation of those who came to Yosemite Valley as tourists. The photographer for the occasion, J. J. Reilly, was capable of far more expressive results when the subject moved him, but he earned his living catering to summertime tourist traffic in the Valley; inevitably, it proved all too easy to simply line the travellers up against that familiar backdrop and be done with them. And so they appear in this oft-repeated pose—casual and secure, with some small artifact to lean upon, their hotel safely in sight, and the surrounding cliffs and waterfalls distantly displayed as if trophies upon a gaming wall. The year is 1875.

As is often the case in photography, larger truths stand revealed through small details. A moment's study of the fence around which the tourists gather reveals that it does not enclose anything—it is simply *there*, a reassuring bit of civilization set in a surround of wildness. Similarly, from the subjects' choice of elegant clothing, and from the photographer's careful inclusion in the picture of one of the few permanent structures in the Valley, we can deduce something of the nineteenth century American intention to conquer the wilderness, rather than to adapt to it. One of the casualties of that conquest would be the Indian, hated perhaps because he occupied the environ-

PLATE 3. J.J. Reilly. *Tourist Party. Ca.1875.*

10

PLATE 2. M.M. Hazeltine. *Mono Indians in Yosemite Valley. Ca.1875.*

ment, but truly doomed because he was an integral part of it.

Unfortunately, photography accentuates our already-existing tendency to view the environment as a myriad of disparate objects, by placing a narrow "frame" around an otherwise vast and continuous panorama. The camera sees through Western eyes, as it were. And so it happens that while we have scores of photographs of individual Indians, of baskets, acorn caches, arrowheads, and so on, we have discouragingly few photographs of Yosemite Indian *life*. To be exact, we have eleven such images, all of them taken by Eadweard Muybridge with a small stereo camera in 1872.

The reality which Muybridge's pictures offer is of a people living in intimate relationship with the land. Their villages were built at the edge of the river, sites chosen both for security and for convenience in fishing and food preparation. The Valley provided many foods, but perhaps its most plentiful offering came from the large groves of oak trees, from which the Indians annually harvested great amounts of acorns. On smooth granite outcroppings near Mirror Lake and elsewhere you can still locate mortar holes where these acorns were ground to flour as a first step in preparing them for eating.

As I note these things, I find it curious that the word *ecology* was not coined until 1873, and remained an obscure branch of the physical sciences for the better part of another century. Yet in this small set of photographs we are offered at least a fragmentary glimpse of the Yosemite Indians as a functioning societal group, a concern far in advance of any formal interest in studying them in this fashion. Actually, Muybridge did not make the pictures for himself, but at the request of painter Albert Bierstadt, who by coincidence was working in

PLATE 4. Kilburn Brothers. *Abandoned Indian Camp, Mono Lake. Ca.1870.*

PLATE 6. Eadweard Muybridge. *Albert Bierstadt's Studio in Yosemite Valley. 1872.*

PLATE 5. Eadweard Muybridge. *A Morning Council on the Merced. 1872.*

Yosemite Valley at the same time, and felt it would be helpful to have some photographic views of common Indian activities to carry back to his San Francisco studio for later reference. One rare image shows Bierstadt himself seated at the edge of the village working at his portable easel, surrounded by attentive Indian children.

Just what use Bierstadt made of these sketches and photographs after returning to his studio is another story altogether. In a Bierstadt painting such as "A Halt in the Yosemite Valley", the cliffs and atmospheric effects have been exaggerated, and the Indians have been transformed; they appear in tailored suits, riding expensive horses with fine saddles, and even (it seems) have along a pack animal and a pet dog. (Historical accuracy, if nothing else, prompts me to note that in general the Indians had only one use for horses—they *ate* them!). Bierstadt has created for us a highly romantic landscape, revealing more about the artist's ideals than about Yosemite itself.

But it has always been within the painter's province to distill and combine a lifetime of personal experience onto a canvas, and the resulting picture is hardly expected to be an example of documentary accuracy. Not so the photograph, at least not in the nineteenth century, when a visually naive public was far more likely to consider a photograph as, literally, a "mirror of reality", and to equate that optical reality with Truth. Realizing this, it is disconcerting to speculate upon the effects of such images as Gustav Fagersteen's "Indian Tom". The elements comprising this photograph, from the Rembrandt-type lighting to the wonderfully subtle grace note in the form of the white horse grazing in the distance, all work together to produce a masterful portrait—but one in which the artificiality of the set-up may not have been apparent to a contemporary observer.

PLATE 7. Gustav Fagersteen. *Indian Tom. Ca.1880.*

PLATE 8. Albert Bierstadt. *A Halt in the Yosemite Valley. Ca.1872.*

There are other photographs, however, which cut through the stereotypes. One such picture, made by Julius Boysen as part of a large series of Indian studies he undertook in the first few years of this century, shows an old Indian, his feet bound in rags. Behind him, the Valley spreads with much of the meadow-like appearance it had before the white men arrived a half-century earlier. But now (1900) he stands in the middle of a wagon road, and far off in the corner of the picture hang four American flags. The Indian's name is Yo-Chak, and he is old. In fact, by 1900 almost all Yosemite Indians were old; after the 1850's "they didn't make Indians anymore", as the saying went, and you can often roughly date a photograph by the age of the Indian in it—the older the Indian, the more recent the photograph. The last full-blooded Ahwahneechee died in 1931.

But the Valley did not change that quickly. It takes a long time for trees to grow, and for hundreds of years the Indians had annually burnt off the underbrush and young pines; in this way they maintained the Valley as largely meadowland (with good vistas for game hunting) and prevented the encroachment of pine forest upon the large stands of oak trees (from which they harvested acorns). That balance was broken with the passing of control of Yosemite to the whites, for whom oak trees were useful only as firewood or lumber, and brushfires simply a threat to their newly-constructed permanent buildings. It was an unequal contest—a tree that had taken a century to grow could be cut down in an hour, and in the process the original inhabitants would be unthinkingly deprived of their dietary staple. And thus the Indians became dependent upon the whites for food and money. And jobs—as domestics, as unskilled laborers.

It is all there, hidden in a casually-made image that tells us far more than was ever recognized by the tourist-trade photographer when he chose that vantage point and that subject and that moment to make his picture. Those unintended details captured so indiscriminately by the lens—a lone oak tree draped with American flags, a wagon road cutting a meadow—reveal relationships out of which the events we call "history" become logical and understandable, and perhaps even inevitable.

PLATE 9. Julius Boysen. *Indian Mary. Ca.1902.*

PLATE 10. Julius Boysen. *Yo-Chak, An Old Indian. 1900.*

The Explorers

Juan Rodriquez Cabrillo, sailing northward along the coast of California in 1542, was the first European to note a range of mountains lying inland from a point opposite the Monterey Peninsula. He spoke of the snow-clad mountains as *las sierras nevadas*—literally, "The Snowy Range"—and soon enough mapmakers working from his descriptions had blocked in a great Sierra Nevada Range. But unfortunately, you can't see the mountains we now call the Sierra Nevada from that point—Cabrillo had simply sighted the nearby chain of Santa Cruz Mountains, topped with a rare blanket of early winter snow. Still, it was hardly a major error compared to the fact that California itself was recorded as an *island* for a very considerable number of decades. Not until 1769, more than two centuries after Cabrillo, did the Spanish make their first overland traverse of California, allowing them to discern at least the general outline of the true Sierra Nevada Range. But having done that, and after making a few other tentative forays, the Spanish were content to let well enough alone; they were neither hunters nor trappers, and knowing nothing of the gold that lay sparkling in the streams of the Sierra foothills, they generally ignored the area.

It remained for American fur trappers and adventurers to carry forward the explorations. Journals kept by a number of these "mountain men", especially among the later Forty-Niners, have been published in recent years, and make for utterly fascinating reading. Equally intriguing to me are the studies that have been made to identify exactly what routes the various explorers took. It is, after all, one thing to follow a road from Bridgeport to Sonora, and quite another to break trail over an unexplored mountain range lying between two as yet nonexistent cities—and then to describe your wanderings in sufficient detail that others can later reconstruct just where you've been! Almost any of those first person accounts contain enough ambiguities (not to mention mutually irreconcilable "facts") to keep a graduate History Department going for a generation or more. A typical entry (in this case from the Walker Expedition of 1833) reads, "We continued our course in the direction of a large mountain, which we could see was covered with snow at its summit. In the evening we camped at the edge of a large lake formed by a river which heads in this mountain. The next day we travelled up this river towards the mountain, where we camped for the night."

One wishes that there could have been a photographer along, for surely just one silver image would tell us which mountain they saw. But even the *invention* of photography was not to come until six years later (in 1839), and it would be another two decades before photographers became an accepted part of such expeditionary ventures. In the interim, we must depend upon the eyewitness descriptions of the participants.

The first crossing of the Sierra by whites came in 1827, when Jedediah Smith led a party of fur trappers across the northern fringe of the range; other groups soon followed, with the mountain passes they used generally named after the leader of the particular expedition. For a comprehensive overview of these explorations, the definitive text is Francis Farquahar's *History of the Sierra Nevada;* it is an impeccably researched and thoroughly engrossing account, and I highly recommend it. But I am interested here primarily in those discoveries which bear directly upon Yosemite, and in that regard the expedition led by Joseph Reddeford Walker, in 1833, overshadows all others in its historical importance.

The Walker expedition of seventy hunters and trappers (and adventurers) set out from the vicinity of the Green River, in Utah, and from there headed directly west, eventually confronting the steep East Side of the Sierra at a point near the present town of Bridgeport, California. As luck would have it, entering the Sierra at that particular point would not serve to bring them over the crest and quickly down the other side, but rather would deposit them on top of the great ridge that separates the canyons of the Tuolumne and Yosemite watersheds. And that is indeed exactly what happened.

To our good fortune, the expedition included as its clerk a young man named Zenas Leonard, who kept a detailed journal of their advance, and wrote at this stage of their crossing, "No one was acquainted with the country, nor knew how wide the summit of the mountain was. We had travelled for five days since arriving at what we supposed to be the summit—were now still surrounded by snow and rugged peaks—the vigor of every man almost exhausted—with nothing to give our poor horses, which were no longer of any assistance to us." But even as he chronicles their increasingly desperate situation, Leonard also enters in his journal a description of some most remarkable terrain they have encountered: "We travelled a few miles every day, still on top of the mountain, and our course contin-

ually obstructed by snow, hills and rocks. Here we began to encounter in our path many small streams which would shoot out from under these high snowbanks, and after running a short distance in deep chasms they have through ages cut through the rock, precipitate themselves from one lofty precipice to another, until they were exhausted in rain below. Some of these precipices appeared to us to be more than a mile high."

Now the Sierra Nevada may abound in "tall mountains" and "large lakes", but no photograph is needed to identify the source of so unique a description as the preceding: it is the northern wall of Yosemite Valley. Being unable to descend the cliffs, however, Walker's party never actually entered the Valley, but only camped upon its rim. In the days that followed the party worked its way into lower (and more benign) country to the west, and at this latter point Leonard mentions, almost in passing, the sighting of "trees of the Redwood species, incredibly large, some of which would measure from 16 to 18 fathoms around the trunk at the height of a man's head above the ground." This is undoubtedly a description of the *Sequoia Gigantea,* another wonder never before seen by the white man.

In due time, Zenas Leonard returned to his parents' home in Pennsylvania and contributed a transcription of his journal to the local newspaper, which published it in serial form, and afterwards in bound book form. Here, then, was the first account of the discovery of Yosemite Valley, written and published—and ignored!—a full generation before the Mariposa Batallion galloped around Artist's Point and beheld that same scene from the opposite wall of the Valley. (Just as a digression, I once came upon a first edition of that early publication, in a used bookstore in San Francisco. Well, I thought elatedly, my years of perusing such places were finally going to prove worthwhile; I was even prepared to sacrifice maybe a hundred dollars, in case the owner already knew what that slim volume represented. Well, yes—he *did* know: it was priced at eleven thousand dollars).

Curiously enough, neither the account of the Walker Expedition of 1833 nor reports from the Mariposa Batallion of 1851 generated an immediate influx of visitors to Yosemite Valley. In fact, but for a small miner's expedition that was reported "ambushed by Indians" under rather suspicious circumstances, and a subsequent Army punitive raid, the Valley was not seen again by white men until 1855. Nonetheless, rumors of a fantastic valley with "a waterfall nearly a thousand feet high" spread from the Mariposa mining community and were bound to reach someone of visionary curiosity sooner or later. As it happened, the person they touched significantly was a young Englishman named James Hutchings, who was already laying plans and gathering material for an illustrated magazine about California life.

Intending to provide his readers with "solid information and a sober, common-sense view of topics of interest", Hutchings brought a photographer with him whenever possible on his travels, so that the most accurate of original images would be available for engravers to work from in preparing illustrations for his magazine. In 1855, however, photography was still an exacting and complicated process, relatively untested—and hence unpredictable—under wilderness working conditions; and so when Hutchings undertook that summer to lead the first "tourist party" into Yosemite Valley, he conservatively invited along a traditional artist, Thomas Ayers, to make pencil sketches that would serve the same illustrative purpose. He could hardly have made a better choice.

Thomas Ayers' sketches, executed in soft pencil, record with fidelity not only the proportions of the cliffs and waterfalls, but also the much less tangible sense of *scale* of the Valley. The artistic devices used to achieve this are evident from a study of the ten surviving sketches now housed at the Yosemite Museum: nearer objects are delineated in sharp, darker pencil, and distant objects in lighter and softly diffuse tones, thus conveying the impression of atmosphere and distance. Small objects of known size—people, horses, tents—are placed discreetly within the frame, thereby providing a visual yardstick for judging the scale of the surrounding scenery. And finally, even the nearest foreground objects generally appear several hundred feet away, minimizing the size distortions of nearby objects and yielding a stately and monumental quality to he Valley and its enclosing cliffs. The limits and subjectivity of the artist are really evident only in the garden-like "artistic" arrangement of foliage, and in a certain softening of the form of the granite cliffs (thereby partially obscuring their geological structure). When the first issue of *Hutchings' California Magazine* appeared the following year, its lead article was "The Yo-Ham-i-te Valley", illustrated with Ayers' sketches, and bringing evidence of the existence of Yosemite Valley to a large audience for the first time.

Science followed Art into the Sierra shortly thereafter in the form of the California State Geological Survey, established by the State Legislature in 1860, and with one Josiah Whitney as its Director. Whitney first set about enlisting competent help for the fieldwork, and to his endless credit acquired some of the most talented and creative spirits one could hope for—among them William Brewer, Charles Hoffman, James Gardner, and Clarence King.

PLATE 11. Thomas Ayers. *Yosemite Valley. 1855.* This was the first sketch made of Yosemite.

PLATE 13. Thomas Ayers. *Vernal Fall. 1855.*

PLATE 12. Thomas Ayers. *The Great Falls. 1855.*

PLATE 14. Thomas Ayers. *In Yosemite Valley. 1855.*

Their work began in December, 1860, continuing intensively through the next four years and on a reduced scale for several more. The results were impressive. The maps drawn by Charles Hoffman set a standard for excellence that would not be equalled until the work of Francois Matthes appeared, well into this century. William Brewer and Clarence King both wrote engaging books recounting their personal exploits—*Up and Down California in 1860-1864,* and *Mountaineering in the Sierra Nevada,* respectively (both works have appeared in paperback editions in recent years). J. D. Whitney prepared the official Reports of the Survey, which culminated in 1868 with the publication of *The Yosemite Book,* a large-format book limited to 250 copies and containing the written conclusions of the Survey, two large fold-out maps of Yosemite and the surrounding Sierra Nevada, and twenty-eight *original* photographs; a year later the same material (but without the photographs) was condensed into a pocket-sized *Yosemite Guide-book,* which proved quite popular with the public and remained in print for many years.

Josiah Whitney was himself an intriguing, if not altogether likeable, figure. Like almost everyone who visited Yosemite, he was curious as to the Valley's origin. Reasoning by a process of comparative example, he ruled out its formation through any of the usual geological forces such as stream erosion or folding strata; he also took particular pains to ridicule as "absurd" the theory of glacial action for its formation. But finally, having ruled out *all* the familiar geological forces that might yield a wide, flat valley surrounded by nearly-vertical, three-thousand foot high cliffs, Whitney was forced to devise a radical hypothesis—that the Yosemite Valley was formed at some cataclysmic moment when the *bottom dropped out* from underneath that section of the Sierra Nevada!

PLATE 15. W. Harriss. *Summit of Mount Hoffman. 1867.* The small figure standing by the surveyor's transit is Hoffman. Nineteenth century explorers had no qualms about naming the most impressive landmarks after themselves, and thus Mt. Brewer and Mt. Hoffman appear prominently on Sierra maps. But rank has its privileges, and Josiah Whitney, as Director of the Geological Survey, modestly reserved the very highest mountain for himself; it must have been a bit embarrassing when it became clear he initially picked *the wrong peak,* and had to return the following year and re-name everything! (It seems poetic justice that the peak he first chose is still referred to by backpackers as "False Mt. Whitney").

PLATE 16. W. Harriss. *State Geological Survey Party at Tuolumne Soda Springs. 1867.*

In fairness to Whitney, one has to remember that his theory did interlock in a general way with the then-popular "convulsive theory" of creation, and also that most any theory of the formation of Yosemite Valley had to lean heavily upon deductive reasoning since so little data about the area had yet been collected. (I am reminded of a *Charlie Brown* cartoon in which Charlie Brown explains to Lucy that in the old days people believed that the Earth was flat and that if they sailed too far out on the ocean they would fall off the edge. Lucy replies, "Ha! Ha! Ha! Boy, that's really dumb! How could they possibly believe anything that stupid?" Then, after a short pause, she adds, "What do we believe now?")

In the end, Whitney's own pride and stubbornness led him to commit a sin unpardonable for a scientist: he became more committed to a particular theory than to the underlying scientific *method* which subjects every theory to the constant test of corroboration by each succeeding piece of evidence. Whitney had come to the Sierra armed with the examples his education and travels had given him, and so he looked for (and usually found) evidence of similar forces at work in the mountains of California. But when, as in this instance, the form of Yosemite Valley differed significantly from that of glacier-filled valleys he had seen in Europe, he eliminated glaciers as a possible shaping force. Stating categorically that "nothing more unlike the real work of ice, as exhibited in the Alps, could be found", Whitney was blind to any evidence to the contrary, and spent the remaining twenty years of his life doggedly defending an increasingly tenuous position.

John Muir, who had proposed the counter-theory that the Valley was slowly carved by the passage of glaciers, reached his conclusions by an entirely different process of reasoning. Muir lived in Yosemite almost continuously from 1868 to 1873, devoting his time to patiently examining each minute aspect of the Sierra landscape for such meaning as it would yield, and then deriving overall theories from the phenomena actually observed. It was a slow process—not the approach to take if you had deadlines to meet, jobs to justify—but the results were cumulative, and Muir was unwaveringly prepared to devote a lifetime to the undertaking. Over the years, he was able to explain the evolution of Yosemite Valley and all of the Sierra Nevada in terms of an orderly process of change in which *all* elements, from the thundering waterfall to the most fragile wildflower, were interconnected. Moreover, he described this with a force and eloquence that disarmed his critics and captivated countless readers who would never have expected to find themselves concerned with the fate of glaciers and water ouzels.

PLATE 17.

PLATE 18. Eadweard Muybridge. *Ancient Glacier Channel at Lake Tenaya. 1872.*

The nineteenth century was, indeed, a momentous age in which to participate in the advance of the natural sciences. Muir's discoveries were made with tools no more elaborate than a notebook, a keen eye, and the simplest of readily available instruments. Moreover, his investigations ranged freely across the disciplines of botany, biology, geology, and more, while his need to give expression to his beliefs and discoveries led him into literature and into the founding of the conservation movement as we know it today. It was a last great opportunity to be both specialist and generalist, before the appreciation for the underlying interdependence of all facets of nature was lost in a sea of increasingly specialized sciences, each requiring enormously expensive and intricate equipment with which to search for amino acids or charmed quarks or black holes.

In recent years the need for an interdisciplinary approach to relate these seemingly disparate facts has become increasingly apparent and urgent. Rachel Carson's *Silent Spring* provided perhaps the most dramatic turning point, drawing upon and relating facts as seemingly mutually exclusive as the non-biodegradable nature of DDT, the structure of the ornithological food chain, the decline of the peregrine falcon population—and the inevitable implications of all this for man. The approach and attitudes illuminated in the works of Muir and Thoreau have been followed more directly in writings such as *The Desert Year* by Joseph Wood Krutch, and *Pilgrim at Tinker Creek* by Annie Dillard. Muir's own writings were extensive, even allowing for duplication and overlapping of material published in different forms over the years. *My First Summer in the Sierra, The Mountains of California,* and *The Yosemite* are all available in paperback, along with numerous anthologies. The quality of the writing is consistently superb—where other books will outline the history of the area, Muir offers you its *meaning.*

PLATE 19. Anon. *Portrait of John Muir.*

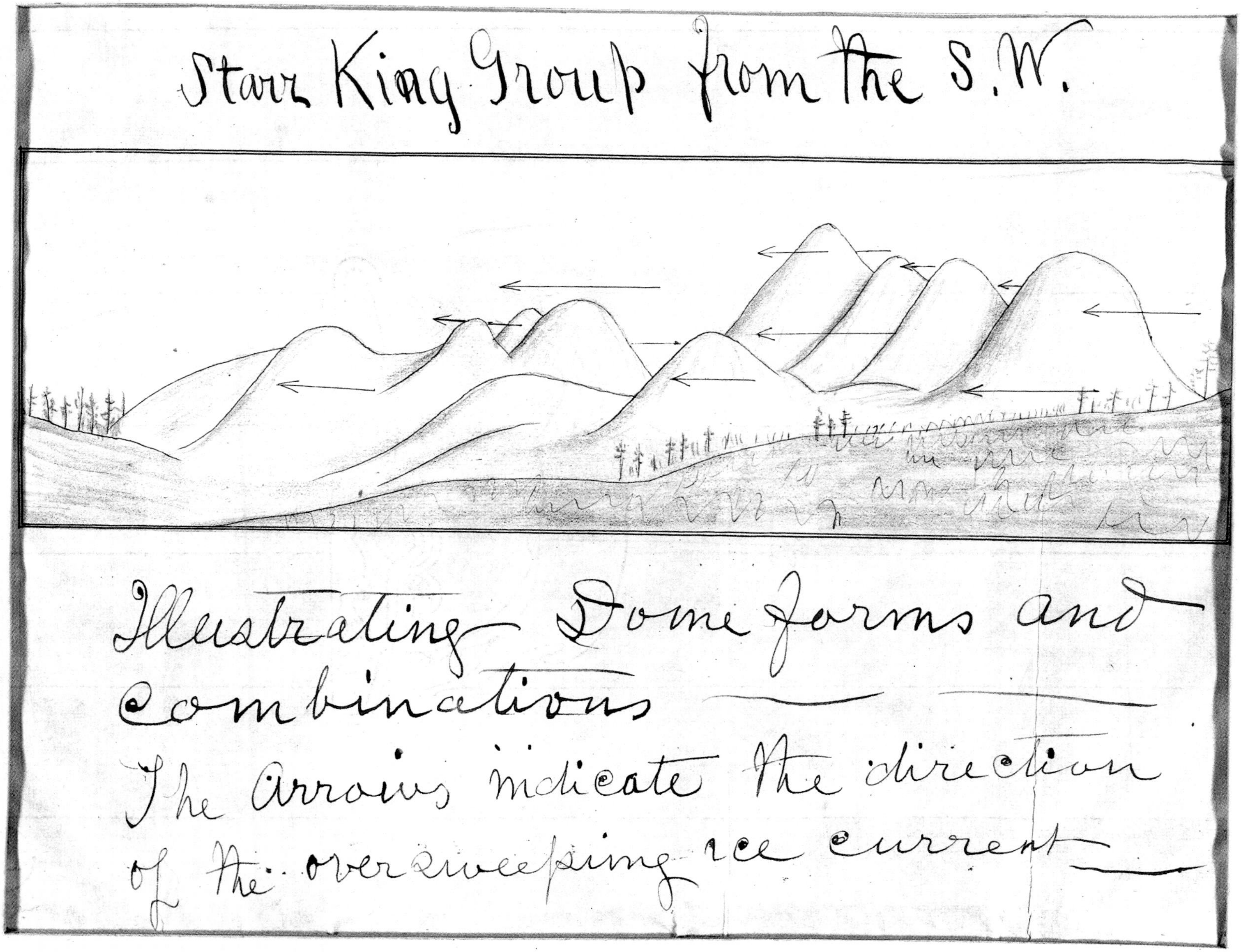

Starr King Group from the S.W.

Illustrating Dome forms and combinations

The Arrows indicate the direction of the oversweeping ice current

PLATE 20. John Muir. *Starr King Group from the S.W. Ca. 1872.* Pen and ink sketch.

Settlers and Tourists

What continually surprises me about Yosemite is that even today it remains in remarkably pristine condition, that while the presence of man has obviously changed the Valley, it has not corrupted it. This is not a small thing to be thankful for, when you consider that a similarly spectacular natural wonder—Niagara Falls—exists today as a perverse spectacle (with colored lights on the Falls at night) surrounded by pollution and tawdry commercialism. That Yosemite should have survived at all is the result of both the large forces of history and the thoughtful actions of a few individuals.

Yosemite was not opened to development until late in the history of our westward expansion; already a public awareness was developing for the need to preserve significant wilderness areas from exploitation, and in 1864 President Lincoln signed a bill setting aside Yosemite Valley and Mariposa Big Trees "for public use, resort and recreation . . . inalienable for all time". A detailed account of the personalities and lobbying that led to passage of the Yosemite Grant may be found in Hans Huth's *Nature and the American: Three Centuries of Changing Values.* Also, while the bill related specifically to Yosemite, it had the wider significance of placing the whole concept of wilderness preservation within a firm legal framework. Thus the creation seven years later of the first National Park—Yellowstone—was a direct outgrowth of the Yosemite legislation.

But if the Yosemite Grant provided the general guidelines for the future use of the area, it remained for private concessionaires to determine the level of taste and commercialism that would actually prevail. And in this respect it was James Hutchings who emerged as the dominant figure in Yosemite affairs from the time of his first visit in 1855 until his death in 1902.

James Mason Hutchings was born in England in 1818, emigrated to America at fifteen, and joined the Gold Rush to California in 1849. In the goldfields he made his first fortune—not, however, from discovering gold. Instead, he published "The Miner's Ten Commandments", a letter-sheet with text and eleven woodcuts, which sold nearly 100,000 copies upon its publication in 1853. Buoyed by the success of this first publishing venture, he brought out additional letter-sheets illustrating "Mining Scenes", "The California Indians" and "The Mammoth Trees". Next came his *California Magazine,* which ran monthly from 1856 to 1861, at which time he gathered the best of its offerings and published them in book form as *Scenes of Wonder and Curiosity in California.*

In 1862 Hutchings settled permanently in Yosemite, and in the years following played a central role in nearly all facets of Yosemite life; he was an energetic climber, operated a hotel, and continued his efforts at publicizing the Valley for tourist travel. All these activities and more were described in his greatest literary effort, *In The Heart of The Sierras.* It was a large book—496 pages—and many of the illustrations were once again drawn from Hutchings' earlier publications, but for the first time he also added twenty full-page photographic plates, repro-

HUTCHINGS'
CALIFORNIA MAGAZINE.

Vol. IV.   OCTOBER, 1859.   No. 4.

THE GREAT YO-SEMITE VALLEY.

CHAPTER I.

How it came to be Discovered.

"I see you stand like grayhounds in
the slips,
Straining upon the start. The game's
a foot;
Follow your spirit; and, upon this
charge,
Cry"—Ho! for the Yo-Semite!

THE early California resident will remember that during the spring and summer of 1850, much dissatisfaction existed among the white settlers and miners on the Merced, San Joaquin, Chowchilla, and Frezno rivers and their tributaries, on account of the frequent robberies committed upon them by the Chook-

THE YO-SEM-I-TE FALL, TWO THOUSAND FIVE HUNDRED FEET IN HIGHT.
[*From a Photograph by C. L. Weed.*]

PLATE 21.   31 duced through the newly-invented process of photo-lithography. These latter reproductions speak well for nineteenth century craftsmanship, for they are virtually indistinguishable in tone and detail from original photographic prints. All things considered, *In The Heart of The Sierras* is the single most important (not to mention enjoyable) account of the early history of Yosemite.

While Hutchings was the most prominent of Yosemite's early citizens, there was another—Galen Clark—who partook equally (though less visibly) in the changes of that first half-century. Galen Clark was already thirty-nine years old when the lure of gold drew him to California, and more specifically into the Mariposa mining community, in 1853. But after two years of rigorous work, he suffered a "hemorrhage of the lungs", which was diagnosed as tuberculosis, an affliction generally fatal in those days. Leaving Mariposa, Clark went up into the mountains, settling in and building a cabin at the place we now call Wawona, there to await the end. The end, as it turned out, was somewhat more than a half-century distant, and Clark used the grace period to full advantage.

In 1857 he entered the Mariposa Grove of Big Trees, exploring and publicizing for the first time an area that had been sighted by white men only once before. When photographer C. E. Watkins toured the Grove in 1861, he photographed Clark standing against the largest of his mammoth tree discoveries, "The Grizzly Giant"; it was a pose repeated innumerable times over the years by Clark, who eventually came to appear as permanent (and almost as old) as the trees themselves.

In 1868, John Muir stopped at Galen Clark's rough-hewn hotel at Wawona while enroute to Yosemite for the first time, and struck a friendship that was to last a lifetime. A few years later Muir and Clark together made the

PLATE 22. Carleton Watkins. *The Grizzly Giant. 1861.*

PLATE 23. Julius Boysen. *The Tunnel Tree, Mariposa Grove, 1902.* With Galen Clark (on the right) posing with a group of tourists. The hole was cut through the tree in 1881, but the tree survived nearly another century before falling sometime during the winter of 1968–9. (Since there was no one in the Grove during the winter to witness its fall, it is not known whether it made a noise . . .)

first exploration of the Tuolumne Canyon, a trip Muir describes in *The Yosemite,* admiring Clark for his strength and daring in fording the Tuolumne River by bounding across boulders submerged beneath the rapids. (Indeed, Clark seemed to gain strength as he grew older, and I found it personally heartening to learn that of the four small books he wrote about Yosemite, the first one was not finished until he was past ninety—a fact which gave me hope that *this* small book would eventually be completed!) But finally, while Clark was in Los Angeles in 1910 to visit his publisher, he took a chill from overdoing it at the nearby Santa Monica Hot Baths, and at age ninety-six that old weakness of the lungs finally caught up with him. Looking back, John Muir's tribute to Clark, not lightly bestowed, seems the simplest and most fitting: "Galen Clark was the best mountaineer I ever met."

Only slowly, though certainly with increasing frequency, did that period of mountaineering make way for more business-minded souls. At first, the veneer of civilization was clearly very thin—the present one-hour drive from Mariposa to Yosemite Valley took two *days* then, and there really were grizzly bears out there in the meadows. The dichotomy is well illustrated in such scenes as Gustav Fagersteen's photograph of a camping party at Bridalveil Fall; a careful examination of the original print reveals several quite large shotguns distributed amongst the more genteel trappings of fine clothing and furniture and pets.

The development of the Valley, in the form of hotels and other concessions, was directly linked to equivalent improvements in the transportation network that served the area. Within the Valley, the earliest "scenic" trails were built to Mirror Lake and Vernal Fall sometime before 1864. Several others were completed as toll-trails in the years following, including the famous Four Mile

PLATE 24. M.M. Hazeltine. *Camping Out Near Ribbon Falls, Yosemite. Ca.1870.* Stereograph. Wilderness photographer Dave Bohn tells me this is a black bear, not a grizzly. [YNP]

opposite:
PLATE 25. Gustav Fagersteen. *Camping Party at Bridalveil Fall. Ca.1880.*

Trail, which at the time provided the only access to Glacier Point's incredible vista of both the Valley and the High Sierra. A photograph made along that trail during its construction shows Yosemite's master trailbuilder, John Conway (seated, far right), with his crew during a lunch break. The size of the crew indicates an undertaking of larger magnitude than we might otherwise suppose; even more surprising, for those of us accustomed to minimizing weight and just nibbling munchies on the trail, is the staggering amount of cast iron cooking paraphernalia the trail crew has with them.

By 1886 the State had lent its financial hand, buying out the toll-trails and making them free, but a carryover from the earlier time may still be noted along the Vernal Fall trail. Along that path, the present junction of the Mist Trail and the horse trail is marked by a house-sized piece of talus still referred to as "Register Rock", so called because it marked the spot where tourists stopped to register and pay their tolls. An 1870 stereograph by Watkins shows the Rock and tollhouse—and, upon closer examination, quite a bit of graffiti upon the Rock!

Of course getting to the Valley in the first place was another problem altogether. The first white men simply followed the Indian trails, but a problem soon arose, for the Indians travelled only on foot, and their paths were unrelated to the requirements of horses. To remedy this, a toll-trail was constructed from Mariposa to Yosemite in 1856, following existing Indian trails at first, but after passing Wawona, veering away from the sheltered forest to the higher elevations where alpine meadows could supply grass to feed the stock. One result of taking this route was that the panoramic "Inspiration Point" view of Yosemite Valley lay far above the now-familiar turnout of the same designation; another was that the precipitous

PLATE 26. Carleton Watkins. *Register Rock. Ca.1875.*

PLATE 27. J.J. Reilly. *Mess House of the Yosemite Valley Trail Builders. Ca.1875.*

descent from that point to the Valley floor provided a terrifying experience for the unprepared tourist. Also, contrary to what we might assume today, horseback riding was *not* a universal skill in the days preceding the automobile; for a variety of reasons, many people were accustomed to riding only in carriages. Given this fact, along with the lurid accounts of the difficulties of a pack-train ride — especially for women, who were expected to wear skirts and ride side-saddle! — it is amazing that twenty years passed between the discovery of Yosemite and construction of the first wagon road into the Valley. But finally, in 1874-75, three wagon roads were completed into Yosemite Valley, and the floodgates were open.

Visitors to Yosemite totalled 42 in 1855, 2,400 in 1875, and 10,000 in 1905. Compared to the present deluge — close to two million annually — the numbers were minescule, yet in some ways their impact upon Yosemite was more disruptive than the greater numbers are now. In fairness, it should be noted that sensibilities were also different then — the environment had yet to become visibly saturated by pollution, and Yosemite's physical isolation made it seem logical to harvest food for the visitors and feed for the horses and lumber for construction right in the Valley rather than carrying it all in. As a result, businesses there in the nineteenth century included fenced-in dairy farms and hayfields, a slaughterhouse, a sawmill owned by Hutchings and operated by none other than John Muir, and the predictable stores and hotels. (Now the question of good taste is another matter. Regarding the hotels, Ansel Adams pointed out to me the curious fact that as each new hotel was constructed, the site chosen was upstream from those already built. The reason for this, he added, was that in those days all the raw sewage was dumped directly into the Merced River, giving a certain competitive advantage to being farthest upstream, since all the others...well, you get the idea).

Unravelling the tangled history of public administration and private concessionaires in Yosemite is difficult at best, and the

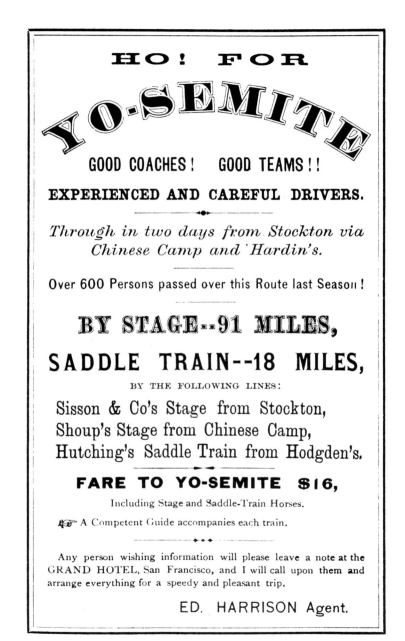

PLATE 28. *Newspaper advertising cut. Pre–1875.*

PLATE 29. George Fiske. *Inbound Stage on the Wawona Road. Ca.1885.*

PLATE 31. Julius Boysen. *Ice Cutters at Mirror Lake. Ca.1901.*

PLATE 30. Julius Boysen. *The Big Tree Room, Cedar Cottage. Ca.1900.*

whole story has never been told well. At present the only book attempting an overview of the topic is Carl P. Russell's now-dated *One Hundred Years in Yosemite*, which plods methodically ahead through two hundred pages of facts without ever stumbling upon an idea. Local Yosemite authors Shirley Sargent and Hank Johnston have achieved somewhat better results with a series of small topical books devoted to such sub-headings as Wawona, Camp Curry, Galen Clark, Yosemite's Famous Visitors, and Women of Yosemite. These small books, self-published under the banner *Flying Spur Press*, are among the few truly indigenous offerings you can buy in Yosemite gift shops; sadly, their low-key design often fights a losing battle in the bookracks against the glossy color picture-books produced by the mass-market souvenir industry. I'd like to think that an inspired account of Yosemite's entire history of commericial/administrative development will appear someday, but I sometimes fear that researching such information is inherently mind-dulling, involving as it does mounds of dusty paperwork shuffled between government clerks (who were just following orders) and small businessmen (who were just following profits).

It turns out there is also an apparently limitless supply of dull photographs, but researching photographs offers one redeeming difference: while you soon despair of ever discovering a Shakespearean sonnet while cataloging interdepartmental memos, you stand a genuine chance of uncovering a truly elegant silver image in a pile of faded snapshots. After all, most photographs are taken because the photographer has felt a genuine emotional response to the scene before him; and even the most amateur among us can point to a few serendipidous examples in which our initial response continues to shine through in the finished print.

How can this be? Why do snapshots by "anonymous" photographers so often compare favorably with photographs made by "professionals"? (This, by the way, has bothered the art establishment ever since the invention of photography, and

has always left the medium slightly suspect in the eyes of purists). One answer, valid both for making and viewing images, has something to do with trusting our intuition. The sense of rapport we feel for our surroundings at certain moments comes most easily when we disengage rational ideas about which particular objects in the scene are worth analyzing, and allow *all* the surrounding elements to be viewed together for the overall pattern they form. And it turns out that the photograph, so terribly ambiguous when asked to tell a specific "story", is incredibly well-suited to revealing a general pattern. The impartial eye of the camera simply bypasses the filter of left-hemisphere logic, and yields a direct view of our surroundings: unaltered, uncensored, unabridged — and often unexpected! From there it is just a matter of visual literacy — you need not know the specific "story" of why that man is atop Glacier Point in his Locomobile in order to understand that his reality, and his relationship to the Land, is profoundly different from that of the old Indian who closed the first chapter of this book.

opposite:
PLATE 32. Anonymous. *The View From Glacier Point. 1900.* The automobile, a ten-horsepower Locomobile, was the first to successfully negotiate the steep dirt roads into Yosemite. (As might be expected, the drivers came from Los Angeles). Park officials, however, were unimpressed with the "blunt-nosed mechanical beetles" (as John Muir affectionately called them), and soon refused to allow any more into the Park; they didn't lift the ban until 1913, and even then subjected horseless carriages to a five dollar entry fee and a speed limit of ten miles per hour.

The Images They Left

Yosemite Valley is a rarity among the popular and accessible natural wonders of the world, from the standpoint that it was discovered by the white man *after* the invention of photography. As a result, there exists a nearly continuous photographic record of our relationship with this wilderness area. From certain vantages such as Union Point, the Valley has been photographed again and again over the years, and the successive images—each recording the same space at a different point in time—can be viewed sequentially, almost like a time-lapse motion picture, to reveal the changing character of the Valley. You watch as forests progressively overrun meadows; roads widen or move or disappear; buildings appear, sprout additions, burn down; and people come, bearing rifles or Frisbees or hoopskirts or motorcycles, And, in a more intimate way, these pictures form a perspective of things lost, of moments forgotten, of changes that—like the growth of a forest—pass too slowly for us to see.

At first, the specific dating and placing of these pictures seems an impossible task, for the notations that accompany them are often obscure if not totally nonexistent. (My favorite is a view labelled only "Misc. Trail Beside Misc. River"). In addition, photographers often failed to identify prints as their own, or, worse yet, would trade negatives with each other as a way to round out their respective offerings. In this manner, for instance, C. E. Watkins bought about three hundred negatives of northern California scenes photographed by A. A. Hart, and reissued them under his own imprint. But then, a few years later,

PLATE 33. Ted Orland. *The Lower Valley From Union Point. 1974.*

PLATE 34. Carleton Watkins. *The Lower Valley From Union Point.*
Ca. 1867. Mammoth Plate.

I. W. Taber acquired many of Watkins' negatives at auction (in a forced bankruptcy sale) and proceeded to reprint them under *his* name. A formidable attempt to determine the authorship of such photographs, and to understand the artistic premises guiding the photographers who made them, has been undertaken by Weston Naef in the elegantly printed book, *Era of Exploration.*

In the special case of Yosemite, if one has the perseverence to compare a large enough selection of prints, it is possible to "bracket" them chronologically, often to the exact year and specific photographer. For example, we know with a certainty that the very first photographs made in Yosemite were taken in 1859 by Charles L. Weed. The occasion for this was another visit to Yosemite by James Hutchings, who was preparing a new series of articles about the area for his *California Magazine,* and brought Weed along to record the scenery, and the new hotel, for illustrations. A study of the resulting photographs shows that Weed ranged widely over the area, carrying his equipment as far as the base of Nevada Fall, and even making the lengthy trip to Mariposa Big Trees to photograph "The Grizzly Giant". Altogether, Weed made about twenty large 10x13 inch negatives and forty stereographs, all of them uniformly mediocre.

Many of the shortcomings were technical rather than artistic—a fact made clear when Weed returned to Yosemite in 1865 and produced a large set of often-impressive images. Unfortunately, many photographs from that trip can be attributed to Weed only on the basis of circumstantial evidence, for he almost never signed his prints, and his stereographs all carried the imprint of Thomas Houseworth, a commercial distributor who published the work of numerous photographers without giving them the benefit of a credit line.

PLATE 35. Charles Weed. *Upper Hotel, 1859.* For many years this was thought to be the first photograph Weed made in Yosemite Valley, based on the fairly straightforward evidence that everyone who was there said so. Historians are a clever lot, though, and by studying the length and direction of shadows appearing in other images made during his initial outing, they now suggest that before taking this picture Weed first tried out his camera on a view of Yosemite Fall. I'll leave the decision to you — there are some questions of history I would willingly dedicate my time to resolving, but I don't care to dance with the angels on the head of *that* particular pin.

PLATE 36. Charles Weed. *Mirror Lake. 1865.*

Historians have largely ignored Charles Weed, partly because his efforts in Yosemite were quickly surpassed by those of Carleton E. Watkins, who began photographing there two years after Weed, in 1861. On his early trips to Yosemite, I often fancy Watkins carrying along a set of Weed stereographs for reference, for frequently his pictures were made from vantage points identical to those chosen by Weed. And whenever their similar views are compared, one can always find some detail—a missing tree branch, for instance—to prove that in every case Weed was there first. Unhappily for Weed, however, Watkins "copies" were superior to Weed's "originals".

Artistically, Watkins invariably improved upon Weed's compositions through subtle changes in vantage point and better use of light and shadow to reveal shapes and planes. And technically, Watkins did no less than revolutionize nineteenth century landscape photography. Prior to about 1900, methods for making enlarged prints had not been perfected, and so the size of the print obtained was the same as the size of the negative—if you wanted a big print, you carried a big camera, and if you wanted a small, album-sized print, you carried a small camera. Most photographers, therefore, carried several cameras with them, ranging in size from a 3½x7 inch stereo camera, up to the accepted maximum size of about 10x13 inches. At least, that was the maximum size until Watkins arrived in Yosemite in 1861 bearing a *mammoth* camera (as historians later called the breed) capable of making 18x22 inch negatives. Suddenly, all the detail and grandeur and overwhelming scale of the great Sierra landscape were within reach of the photographer. Watkins' mammoth-plate views of Yosemite became the standard against which all others were measured; the prints received international awards, and a set was circulated in Congress in 1864 to garner support for passage of the Yosemite Act.

PLATE 37. Charles Weed. *Yosemite Valley, From Mariposa Trail. 1865.* Stereograph.

PLATE 38. Carleton Watkins. *First View From the Mariposa Trail. 1866.* Stereograph.

48

PLATE 39. Carleton Watkins. *Yosemite Valley, First View From the Mariposa Trail. Ca.1867.* Mammoth Plate.

PLATE 40. Carleton Watkins. *The Merced River and Lower Valley. Ca.1867*. Mammoth Plate.

PLATE 41. Carleton Watkins. *The Domes of Yosemite. Ca.1867.* Mammoth Plate.

It was a great conceptual leap forward to envision the artistic effect of a mammoth-sized photograph of wilderness, but there still remained very tangible problems to overcome in putting the idea into practice. In 1861 there were only crude trails leading to Yosemite, necessitating travel on horseback and, in Watkins' case, an accompanying twelve-mule packtrain to carry his equipment and supplies. When the caravan would come upon a promising scene, the five mules carrying the photographic equipment had first to be unpacked, and a portable darkroom assembled. The need for the darkroom derived from the then-current photographic technology, which required that the sensitized plate be manufactured on the spot at the time the picture was about to be made. So Watkins would slip into his developing tent and balance a two-pound sheet of glass in one hand, while pouring the syrupy "collodion" emulsion over its surface with the other. This was no small trick, for the photographer had to tilt the glass back and forth in the semi-darkness in such a way that the collodion flowed *evenly* over the entire 18x22 inch surface—otherwise the resulting negative would be marred by streaking. When the collodion had dried to the point of tackiness, the plate was placed in the waiting camera, there to be exposed for a few minutes to an hour or more, depending upon the light. But that was only the halfway point, for it was also in the nature of the "wet plate process", as it was called, that the plate had to be developed *before the emulsion dried,* or else it lost all sensitivity to the developing process. And so Watkins would disappear once more into that little tent, hopefully to emerge later with a useable negative. The processing done, he could then repack all his equipment and head on around the bend to the next view—and start all over again.

PLATE 42. *Bridalveil Fall. Ca.1867.* Mammoth Plate. While this image is attributed to Watkins, the appearance of a small figure perched jauntily on the rock in the foreground is disconcertingly characteristic of Weed's style. Watkins virtually never included a figure in the scene.

PLATE 43. Carleton Watkins. *Bridalveil Fall. Ca.1867.* Mammoth Plate.

For a variety of reasons, very few of the early glass negatives have survived to the present day. Quite apart from the obvious hazards of carrying boxes of window glass around the wilderness on muleback for weeks on end, the photographers themselves often contributed to the early demise of their negatives. Glass was an expensive material then, and if the picture-making process just related did not yield a handsome negative, the photographer simply took a razor blade and scraped off the emulsion so that the glass could be used again. Even when the view turned out well, he was likely to cast a squinty economic eye upon it and say, "Now that's a *twenty print* negative!", and scrape off the image after printing that many. And finally, the necessity of processing film in the field—perhaps using muddy stream water, or bucketfuls of snow melted over a fire—was hardly conducive to producing negatives of archival permanence, free from stains and subsequent fading.

Somehow, Watkins managed to survive these forms of attrition relatively unscathed, only to run headlong into major disasters later on. The first of these was the financial panic of 1873-74, during which his business failed, and creditors seized most of the prints and negatives he had produced over the preceding twelve years—including more than a hundred mammoth plates, and two thousand stereographs, of Yosemite. This left Watkins in the unenviable position of not only having to re-produce all his Yosemite views, but also finding himself in competition with his own earlier work, which was being reissued under the imprint of his foreclosing creditor, I. W. Taber. But Watkins did gamely return to Yosemite the following year, labelling all his subsequent work there "Watkins' New Series". It should also be noted that during his long career, Watkins also undertook major expeditions to

PLATE 44. Carleton Watkins. *Nevada Fall. Ca.1867.*

PLATE 45. Carleton Watkins. *Three Brothers. 1861.*

Oregon and the Pacific Northwest, and completed a valuable series on the California Missions.

Eventually, about 1890, Watkins' eyesight began to fail, and his productive period eased off into retirement. He still retained all the work he had produced since 1875, and was negotiating with Stanford University for its purchase and preservation, when a second and overwhelming disaster struck. On the morning of April 18, 1906, the west side of the San Andreas Fault shifted eight feet to the north, and San Francisco burned to the ground. Incredibly, one poignant and terrifying picture from that morning survives to show Watkins, then seventy-seven years old and nearly blind, being led from his demolished studio as the flames approached to complete the destruction of his entire life's work. Nothing was saved; it was a tragic end to a brilliant career.

Watkins was not alone in making truly magnificent photographs of the Yosemite landscape. In 1867, a handsome set of views of the Valley appeared from a photographer who signed his prints "Helios" (from the Greek word for "sunlight"). San Francisco photographer and gallery owner Eadweard Muybridge announced himself as the Publisher of these views, and wrote of "Helios'" achievement: "For artistic effect, and careful manipulation, they are pronounced by all the best painters and photographers in the city to be the most exquisite photographic views ever produced on this coast". Well, as it turned out slightly after the fact, Eadweard Muybridge *was* "Helios"! The reason for his initial use of a pseudonym has never been explained—perhaps he simply felt it would be too awkward to apply such accolades to himself openly.

In any event, Muybridge—or "Helios"—made a hundred 6½x8½inch plates and 160 stereographs on that

Yosemite Valley, California.
HELIOS,
Cosmopolitan Gallery of Photographic Art,
Montgomery St., San Francisco.

Entered according to Act of Congress, 1868, by E J. Muybridge, in Clerk's Office of Dist. Court U.S., Dist. California.

PLATE 46. Anonymous. *Carleton Watkins being led from his studio by his son Collis, following the San Francisco earthquake on April 18, 1906.* Snapshot.

1867 trip, achieving results that, despite their small size, compared favorably with Watkins' mammoth views. By 1872, Muybridge had himself acquired mastery of the mammoth camera, and sought advance subscription from Patrons of the Art to finance a second trip to Yosemite. His Prospectus stated that "the size of my proposed negatives will be 20x24 inches, and the prints about 18x22, of which subscribers will be entitled, for each one hundred dollars, to select FORTY from the whole series, to be printed and mounted upon India tinted boards". The trip itself was a tremendous success, yielding 51 mammoth plates, 36 6½x8½ inch views, and 379 stereographs. The prints were released to the public the following spring, bringing Muybridge instant acclaim and netting him over twenty thousand dollars profit—all this happening, ironically, at the very time Watkins' business fell into bankruptcy.

In comparing the photographs of Watkins and Muybridge, the most immediately apparent difference lies in the evocation of atmospheric effect in the work of the latter. Such effects were not easily obtained, for the film then used was sensitive only to blue light, with the result that the bright blue sky always printed out as white. At least one pioneer photographer, Timothy O'Sullivan, used this "limitation" to fine advantage as a design and conceptual element in capturing the feeling of the searing desert country of the southwest. In Yosemite, however, a featureless white sky gave the landscape beneath a decidedly bleak appearance, and photographers sought ways to circumvent the problem. The earliest solution was simply to limit the amount of sky that appeared at all, often by using rounded frames that allowed a substantial amount of open sky at the center of the composition, but progressively less toward the edges. An alternative method soon discovered was to make a separate negative of just clouds, and then "print-in" the clouds on top of an otherwise white sky. (The Watkins' landscapes produced as Plates 40 and 41, for instance, both have the *same* cloud above them!) While this approach was in many ways an improvement, there was still a certain lack of verisimilitude in having that same dumpy little Fresno cloud gracing so many Sierra views.

Muybridge likewise often printed-in clouds from separate negatives, but soon he devised a new method that was to yield even better results. Clouds had always been recorded on a separate negative only because the inherent contrastiness of the collodion emulsion was unable to encompass the *range* of brightness typically encountered in the natural landscape—in essence, a short exposure was required for the bright clouds, but a long exposure was needed for the much darker landscape. Muybridge's solution to this impasse took the form of a mechanical "skyshade", an adjustable curtain which hung out in front of the lens and shielded the light from the sky area of the scene from reaching the film during *part* of the exposure, and was then removed for the remainder of the exposure. With this simple device (which Muybridge quickly patented), photographers were for the first time free to include the clouds that were actually *there,* as an integral part of the landscape photograph.

Other artistic differences between the work of Muybridge and Watkins are more subtle, and evident perhaps only from viewing a wider selection of prints than can be included here. In a general way, one could say that Watkins was a Classicist, and Muybridge a Romantic. Watkins would organize his compositions into orderly horizontal and vertical elements, often lacing them together with gently curving lines, all working together to empha-

PLATE 47. Eadweard Muybridge. *Valley of the Yosemite, Early Morning from Moonlight Rock*. Mammoth Plate. *1872*.

PLATE 48. Eadweard Muybridge. *Tenaya Canyon from the Four Mile Trail.* Mammoth Plate. *1872.*

PLATE 49. Eadweard Muybridge. *South Dome. 1872.* Mammoth Plate.

PLATE 50. Eadweard Muybridge. *Edge of Upper Yosemite Falls. 1872.* Mammoth Plate.

PLATE 51. Eadweard Muybridge. *Nevada Fall and Liberty Cap from Glacier Point. 1872.* Mammoth Plate.

size the enduring and harmonious aspects of the Sierra landscape. It was, perhaps, an outgrowth of his work with the Whitney Survey, reflecting his understanding that the primary features of the Sierra landscape existed on a *geologic* time-scale. Muybridge, in contrast, was moved by the drama and change that, in another sense, also pervade the natural scene. Using a wide-angle lens that accentuated differences in scale and distance, he created compositions dominated by jagged diagonals and unexpected outcroppings of rock, often juxtaposed with soft and airy clouds and cliffs in the distance. Even allowing for a good deal of stylistic overlapping—of photographs which might well have been taken by either photographer—it is apparent that their strongest work emphasizes the differences, rather than the similarities, between them. Watkins' best pictures have a certain no-nonsense stateliness about them; the observer (the camera) is securely on the ground, and the planes of the landscape are anchored to a firm horizon. In Muybridge's strongest images, nothing is secure; the observer appears suspended in space, viewing a dynamic and clearly temporal world.

While large prints brought the photographer prestige, the small and ubiquitous stereographs brought in most of the income. The stereo camera required for making these pictures was equipped with two lenses placed about the same distance apart as human eyes, and produced two separate negatives simultaneously on each 3½x7 inch plate. The resulting pictures were then viewed through an optical device called a stereoscope (or stereopticon), which permitted the left image to be viewed only with the left eye, and the right image with the right eye. When the brain integrated the slightly different perspective offered by each picture, the effect was of a single, *fully three-dimensional* scene.

PLATE 52. Eadweard Muybridge. *Self-Portrait on Contemplation Rock, Glacier Point. 1872.*

PLATE 53. Carleton Watkins. *Vernal Fall. Ca.1867.* Mammoth Plate.

PLATE 54. Eadweard Muybridge. *Vernal Fall. 1872.*

Strangely enough, the stereograph, ideally suited to benefit from the infinite amount of detail so easily and accurately captured on film, had been invented two years before the invention of photography itself. The difficulty of mechanically drawing the two images was so great, however, that it remained only a scientific curiosity. But as photography advanced, photographic stereographs became incredibly popular, until by the 1870's no well-to-do Victorian household was without its parlor-room stereoscope and card collection. Watkins and Muybridge catered to this trade by making identical large-plate and stereographic views of each scene, a fairly simple procedure which required only the switching of cameras on the tripod while the processing apparatus remained set up. (Those who followed often took the more expedient route of dispensing with the large views altogether, with a consequent proliferation of the smaller images; one collection I have seen contains over four thousand different stereographs of Yosemite!)

Many stereograph photographers, such as Charles Bierstadt from Niagara Falls, or C. L. Pond from Buffalo, N.Y., maintained studios in the east, but made special trips west to photograph Yosemite. Others, such as J. J. Reilly, simply packed up everything and moved west. Reilly became, in 1875, the first photographer to open a studio in Yosemite; being in poor health, he operated his business with a succession of partners whose names are variously imprinted with his on the stereographs. In all, probably a hundred different commercial photographers had made sets of stereographs in Yosemite before the craze began to fade in the 1880's. The cards they produced exist in wildly varying quantities depending upon the subject and upon the photographer's ability to market his product; or, as one photo historian rather

PLATE 55. C.L. Pond. *The Photographers' Camp at Glacier Point. 1872.* Stereograph. A self-portrait.

opposite:

PLATE 56. C.L. Pond. *Cloud's Rest. 1872.* Stereograph.

PLATE 57. Reilly & Ormsby. *LaMons Cabin, Yosemite Valley, Cal.* Stereograph. Lamon was the first permanent settler in Yosemite Valley, and the first white man to spend the winter there. The latter act required a certain leap of faith, since the prevailing wisdom of the time was that in winter the snow from surrounding mountains drifted down into the Valley, filling it to a depth of several hundred feet! Lamon's cabin has long since disappeared, but the apple trees he planted around it still survive in what has become the overflow parking area for Camp Curry.

AMERICAN SCENERY,

PHOTOGRAPHED BY

C. L. POND,

BUFFALO, N. Y.

628—Summit Peaks of Clouds Rest, 10,450 feet above the sea.

Photographic Views

OF AMERICAN SCENERY.

Reilly & Ormsby,

STOCKTON CAL.

No. 515, La. Mons Cabin, Yosemite, Valley, Cal.

1182. Vernal Falls, 300 ft, high. Yo Semite Val.

PLATE 58. Charles Bierstadt. *Vernal Fall. Ca.1872*. Stereograph

opposite:

PLATE 59. J.J. Reilly & Co. *El Capitan. Ca.1875*. Stereograph.

PLATE 60. Charles Bierstadt. *Mirror View of North & South Dome, Yo Semite Valley Cal. Ca.1872*.

dryly commented, "The photographer's output was limited only by the degree to which he overestimated his audience".

When Reilly departed from the scene about 1880, his last partner, Gustav Fagersteen, inherited his studio and operated it for several more years. Little is known about Fagersteen personally, beyond the fact that he was a German immigrant, but his photographs speak eloquently for his artistic sensitivity. He travelled about the Valley in a covered carriage that doubled as a darkroom, on the back of which was painted in florid script, "Gustav Fagersteen, Artist". His camera was generally a 6½x8½, and the lens he used was exceedingly wide-angle—and hopelessly unsharp. Despite this, he often printed his negatives to their farthest fuzzy corners, and sometimes even beyond that—the picture of the campers shown on page 35 includes a semicircular surround of black so far off-center that the lens failed to record anything at all.

With the appearance of studios in the Valley, there was a corresponding increase in the number of portraits taken there, since the photographer was now in a position to make and deliver prints before the customer left for home again. It is not surprising, therefore, that a large proportion of Fagersteen's pictures were of such groups. *Large* groups, often, for the sales possibilities were then multiplied accordingly. Most of these portraits were taken from the front porch of his studio, with the same backdrop of Upper Yosemite Fall appearing in each picture. The groups extend in a horizontal band across the vertical format, and your eye is drawn in upon them since the image blurs away toward the edges. Fagersteen posed his subjects with great attention to detail, and they sit or stand with a formality or casualness that seems to match their character. The attention to detail is carried further by including in the composition personal belong-

PLATE 61. Gustav Fagersteen. *Yosemite or Bust. 1877.* Stereograph. A self-portrait, with Fagersteen standing beside his darkroom wagon; another view of the wagon reveals the words "Gustav Fagersteen, Artist" painted in florid script across the back.

PLATE 62. Gustav Fagersteen. *Group Portrait, Hunting Party.*
Ca.1880. By mid-summer, Yosemite Fall often dwindle to a mere
trickle, and so here a suitably impressive torrent was *painted in* on
the original negative before printing. Art steps in where nature fails,
as they say.

PLATE 63. Gustav Fagersteen. *Group portrait. Ca.1880.*

PLATE 64. Gustav Fagersteen. *Group portrait. Ca.1880.*

PLATE 65. Gustav Fagersteen. *Group portrait. Ca.1880.*

PLATE 66. Gustav Fagersteen. *Group portrait. Ca.1880.*

ings carried by the subjects, revealing the ways in which these people related—or refused to relate—to the surrounding landscape.

Most of Fagersteen's photographs, and those made by others preceding him into Yosemite, were taken during the summers. By 1880, however, two developments dramatically increased the potential for working there in other seasons. The first of these changes—actually a progressive change that spanned a period of several years—was the establishment of a community of year-around residents in Yosemite Valley; the second development was the invention of a new type of film called the "dry plate", which was presensitized and ready to use anytime, and which could be developed later at the photographer's convenience. The first Yosemite photographer to exploit the possibilities offered by these circumstances was George Fiske, who had visited the Valley in 1872, and returned to live there and establish a studio in 1880.

Fiske perhaps sensed the void that existed in winter views of Yosemite, for during the next two decades he concentrated upon portraying the landscape during that season. Those forays into the snow must have been arduous affairs, even with the new-found mobility that accrued from being able to cram all the necessary equipment into a single "cloud-chasing chariot", as he called it. Fiske's original prints of those winter scenes capture a wondrous amount of detail, and record with great fidelity the high-key values that define the form and texture of the snow. Unfortunately, that is the very subtlety which gets lost in the translation to a halftone illustration on the printed page. Such illustration has been the "Great Equalizer" of photography, levelling every photograph, whether taken with a 35mm or an 18x22 inch mammoth, to the same 150 dots-per-inch of detail and tonal gradation. And once people became accustomed to viewing published illustra-

PLATE 67. George Fiske. *Self-Portrait. Ca.1890.*

PLATE 68. George Fiske. *Yosemite Fall in Winter. Ca.1890.*

PLATE 69. George Fiske. *The Valley in Summer. Ca.1890.*

PLATE 70. George Fiske. *The Valley in Winter. Ca.1890.*

PLATE 71. George Fiske. *Inspiration Point, Winter. Ca.1885.*

tions rather than original prints, the rationale for working with a large camera was, in good measure, lost.

Fiske was the last great Yosemite photographer of the nineteenth century, and when two-thirds of his negatives were destroyed by a fire in 1904, it was clearly the end of an era. Already larger events in the photographic world were making the tourist-oriented studio obsolete. The change took the form of the Eastman Kodak Camera No. 1, introduced in 1888 under the motto, "You Push the Button, We Do the Rest". The claim was hardly an exaggeration: the camera arrived already pre-loaded with a 100-exposure roll of film, and after the hundredth picture had been taken, you packed up the *entire camera* and mailed it back to Rochester, N.Y., where Kodak developed the film, made the prints, reloaded your camera and returned it to you. The process was considerably simplified in 1895 with the introduction of the Kodak No. 2 Camera, which permitted do-it-yourself film loading.

Both these cameras shared the dubious distinction of having lenses even worse than Fagersteen's, but Kodak thoughtfully alleviated the shortcoming by masking off all the fuzzy corners, with the result that the pictures they produced were *circular*. The early hand-cameras also lacked any sort of viewfinder, other than a small arrow stamped on the top of the camera and pointing in the same direction as the lens. But it hardly mattered; the public was delighted at the prospect of assuming the role of photographer, and if the camera was unsuited to making a carefully composed image of the grand landscape, it excelled in capturing those fleeting and personal events important to the Kodaker. The "snapshot"—a wonderfully appropriate term—became the contemporary artform (though we are only now accepting that fact) and the need for a professional photographer in Yosemite faded away.

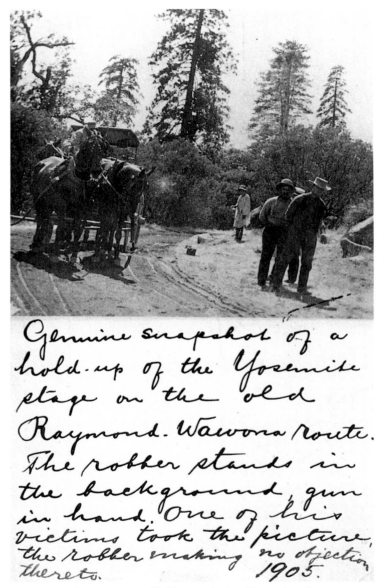

Genuine snapshot of a hold-up of the Yosemite stage on the old Raymond-Wawona route. The robber stands in the background, gun in hand. One of his victims took the picture, the robber making no objection thereto. 1905.

PLATE 72. Anonymous. *Hold-up of the Yosemite Stage.* 1905. Snapshot.

"What fools these mortals be!"
(Overhanging Rock at Glacier Point, 3200
feet above the Valley floor).

PLATE 73. Anonymous. *Mrs. Ralph & Celeste at Glacier Point. 1914.* Photo postcard.

PLATE 74. Anonymous. *At Overhanging Rock, Glacier Point. 1920.* Photo Postcard.

Reality, of course, is never as quite so clean-cut as historians would have us believe. And so, while I do mean to close this account of Yosemite at the entrance to the twentieth century, it seems healthy to allow for a couple of exceptions.

The first is Julius Boysen, who opened a tent-covered studio in the Valley in 1900, and the following season acquired more traditional quarters that he maintained on into the 1920's. Though his period of productivity overlaps that of two other Yosemite studio photographers — Arther Pillsbury and Daniel Foley — Boysen's work shows continued artistic merit, while that of his two contemporaries has long since faded into commercial oblivion.

Boysen never staked a claim to large vistas of Yosemite; instead, like Fiske, he concentrated on subjects which to that time had not been well-documented. For Fiske it was the Valley in winter, for Boysen it was the Mariposa Grove of Big Trees, and the Yosemite Indians. The Indian studies in particular, though obviously contrived in pose and dress, offer the only extended series on the last remaining examples of this tribe. In both series, there is a sense for history, for preserving in silver images a race of people already disappearing, and a grove of trees so primeval one would more likely expect to find a dinosaur than a stagecoach nearby.

The other story briefly luring this text into the twentieth century involves Best's Studio, founded by Harry Best in 1902. Best himself was a well accepted but hardly world-class painter of Yosemite scenes. His real claim upon posterity, however unintentional, results from the unlikely concordance of having had a photofinishing service at his Studio, the only piano in Yosemite Valley, and a stunningly beautiful daughter named Virginia. These circumstances were to prove an exact match for the interests of a somewhat frail, 14-year-old music student (and beginning photographer) who accompanied his parents on their summer vacation trip to Yosemite in 1916. The youngster's name was Ansel Adams.

Adams returned each summer for several years, building his strength by hiking every Sierra trail he could find, practicing the piano, and — with the photofinishing shop close at hand — devoting increasing energy to his photography. (Author Nancy Newhall included a lyrical and extended account of this era of his life in her biography *The Eloquent Light;* her account captures the essence of Adams' personality, which always sparkled with wit and spontenaiety — qualities lost entirely to those who knew him only through his serious and carefully composed images.) In 1928, Virginia became Virginia Best Adams, and a few years later inherited her father's Studio. Boysen and Pillsbury departed the scene about the same time, leaving Yosemite a virtual artistic vacuum for the first time since its discovery; and so Ansel, his future secure with a home in the Valley and a steady income from the Studio Virginia now operated, set out to follow his vision of Yosemite and the Range of Light.

PLATE 75. Anonymous. *Best's Studio. Ca.1905.*

PLATE 76. Julius Boysen. *Self-Portrait. 1901*. Boysen appears here on the left, with his brother and father.

PLATE 77. Julius Boysen. *Indian Woman and Child. 1902.*

PLATE 78. Julius Boysen. *The Fallen Monarch, Mariposa Grove of Big Trees. Ca.1903.*

There is, ideally, no reason why the plurality of worlds encompassed by the snapshot and the view camera should not happily coexist, but more often than not it happens that one reality achieves a temporary dominance by standing atop and crushing another. It is that way with all that has occurred: I think back to the Indians, to the explorers, to the settlers, to the tourists; I think back to the mammoth-plate views, to the stereographs, to the studios, to the snapshots. And as each world passes, I am reminded of something Dante Gabriel Rossetti wrote about the painters who preceded the Renaissance: "They have left little, and but little heed is taken of that which men hold to have been surpassed; it is gone like time gone—a track of dust and dead leaves that merely led to the fountain".

But on close encounter, distinctions between these groups and eras merge and disappear. Were you to wander now, as a John Muir might, along the overgrown trails that first brought the white man to Yosemite, you would discover that everywhere the marks of Time are pressed upon the land. And at some moment the realization comes that you cannot speak simply of a Yosemite as it is *now* or as it was *then*, for continually you find yourself cutting through strata of time, standing upon pieces of earlier eras or eons that Man and Nature have left intact. You could, for instance, park at that familiar Inspiration Point turnout—the one that inspires a million snapshots a year—and by climbing the hillside immediately behind it locate the *first* trail that white men cut into the Valley. That trail, which guided Watkins' twelve-mule caravan in the 1860's, still affords passage for a small but steady stream of summer hikers. And if you were to persevere and follow the trail for an hour or so up the mountainside, you would suddenly emerge upon a large, flat open space — *old* Inspiration Point, scenic turnout for the first stagecoach and (later) auto road that came around the mountain, superceding the horse trail in the 1870's, and itself abandoned when W.P.A. crews rerouted the highway through the mountain via the Wawona Tunnel. The view from this earlier turnout, once extolled on a multitude of stereographs, is now obscured by thirty-foot trees grown through cracks in its asphalt cover, and the turnout itself will likely disappear long before the horse trail it was expected to replace. But that is just the way time shapes things as Man and Nature interact to reach an equilibrium point. Each event, no matter how fleeting, irrevocably alters the course of the future. *We are all part of the process.*

PLATE 79. Ted Orland. *Self-Portrait Atop Half Dome. 1977.*

ILLUSTRATIONS.

Drawn by T. Hill.

PACIFIC PRESS, OAKLAND, CAL.

Sources for the Illustrations are abbreviated as follows:

[YNP]   Yosemite Museum
[NYPL]   New York Public Library
[LACM]   Los Angeles County Museum
[P]   Private Collections

PLATE 1. Ted Orland. *The Yosemite Valley. June 1973.* Even today, when Yosemite often resembles a seven-mile-long summer cruise ship — taking on 30,000 new travellers each weekend — there are still special moments when the magic of the space transcends all... [P]

PLATE 2. M.M. Hazeltine. *Mono Indians in Yosemite Valley. Ca.1875.* Stereograph. [YNP]

PLATE 3. J.J. Reilly. *Tourist Party. Ca.1875.* Stereograph. [P]

PLATE 4. Kilburn Brothers. *Abandoned Indian Camp, Mono Lake. Ca.1870.* Stereograph. [YNP]

PLATE 5. Eadweard Muybridge. *A Morning Council on the Merced. 1872.* Stereograph. [YNP]

PLATE 6. Eadweard Muybridge. *Albert Bierstadt's Studio in Yosemite Valley. 1872.* Stereograph. [P]

PLATE 7. Gustav Fagersteen. *Indian Tom. Ca.1880.* Indian Tom was James Hutchings' domestic help for many years, and details of his life are mentioned in Hutchings' *In The Heart of The Sierras.* [YNP]

PLATE 8. Albert Bierstadt. *A Halt in the Yosemite Valley. Ca.1872.* A steel-line engraving made from a Bierstadt painting for publication in Appleton's Magazine. [P]

PLATE 9. Julius Boysen. *Indian Mary. Ca.1902.* [YNP]

PLATE 10. Julius Boysen. *Yo-Chak, An Old Indian. 1900.* An album of Boysen's Indian studies is preserved in the Yosemite Museum; amazingly enough, the original negative to this image also survives. [YNP]

PLATE 11. Thomas Ayers. *Yosemite Valley. 1855.* This was the first sketch made of Yosemite. [YNP]

PLATE 12. Thomas Ayers. *The Great Falls. 1855.* [YNP]

PLATE 13. Thomas Ayers. *Vernal Fall. 1855.* [YNP]

PLATE 14. Thomas Ayers. *In Yosemite Valley. 1855.* [YNP]

PLATE 15. W. Harriss. *Summit of Mount Hoffman. 1867.* [YNP]

PLATE 16. W. Harriss. *State Geological Survey Party at Tuolumne Soda Springs. 1867.* [P]

PLATE 17. Anon. *Water-Ouzel Diving and Feeding.* A cut from the 1894 edition of Muir's *The Mountains of California*, recently reissued in paperback by Ten Speed Press (Berkeley CA). [YNP]

PLATE 18. Eadweard Muybridge. *Ancient Glacier Channel at Lake Tenaya. 1872.* Mammoth Plate. [YNP]

PLATE 19. Anon. *Portrait of John Muir. Ca.1985.* [YNP]

PLATE 20. John Muir. *Starr King Group from the S.W. Ca. 1872.* Pen and ink sketch. [YNP]

PLATE 21. *Hutchings California Magazine, October 1859.* [P]

PLATE 22. Carleton Watkins. *The Grizzly Giant. 1861.* Stereograph. [P]

PLATE 23. Julius Boysen. *The Tunnel Tree, Mariposa Grove, 1902.* [YNP]

PLATE 24. M.M. Hazeltine. *Camping Out Near Ribbon Falls, Yosemite. Ca.1870.* [YNP]

PLATE 25. Gustav Fagersteen. *Camping Party at Bridalveil Fall. Ca.1880.* [YNP]

PLATE 26. Carleton Watkins. *Register Rock. Ca.1875.* Stereograph. The small tent beneath the Rock is the photographer's darkroom, a necessary accessory to the picture-making process before about 1880. [P]

PLATE 27. J.J. Reilly. *Mess House of the Yosemite Valley Trail Builders. Ca.1875.* Stereograph [P]

PLATE 28. *Newspaper advertising cut. Pre–1875.* This was one of the horse routes into Yosemite prior to the opening of the stage roads. [YNP]

PLATE 29. George Fiske. *Inbound Stage on the Wawona Road. Ca.1885.* [YNP]

PLATE 30. Julius Boysen. *The Big Tree Room, Cedar Cottage. Ca.1900.* Cedar Cottage was an extension to the old Upper Hotel, operated by James Hutchings for many years. Contemporary accounts note that the roof leaked like a sieve around the tree trunk in every storm, the fireplace design often drew the smoke back down the chimney into the room, the hotel itself was situated such that from November to May it was perpetually in the shadow of the surrounding cliffs, and (in the early days) the partitions between the rooms consisted of translucent cheesecloth. Not unlike the present-day tent cabins at Camp Curry, methinks . . .

PLATE 31. Julius Boysen. *Ice Cutters at Mirror Lake. Ca.1901.* [YNP]

PLATE 32. Anonymous. *The View From Glacier Point. 1900.* [LACM]

PLATE 33. Ted Orland. *The Lower Valley From Union Point. 1974.* [P]

PLATE 34. Carleton Watkins. *The Lower Valley From Union Point. Ca. 1867.* Mammoth Plate. [YNP]

PLATE 35. Charles Weed. *Upper Hotel, 1859.* [YNP]

PLATE 36. Charles Weed. *Mirror Lake. 1865.* Mammoth Plate. [NYPL]

PLATE 37. Charles Weed. *Yosemite Valley, From Mariposa Trail. 1865.* Stereograph. [P]

PLATE 38. Carleton Watkins. *First View From the Mariposa Trail. 1866.* Stereograph. [P]

PLATE 39. Carleton Watkins. *Yosemite Valley, First View From the Mariposa Trail. Ca.1867.* Mammoth Plate. [YNP]

PLATE 40. Carleton Watkins. *The Merced River and Lower Valley. Ca.1867.* Mammoth Plate. [YNP]

PLATE 41. Carleton Watkins. *The Domes of Yosemite. Ca.1867.* The cloud appearing in this picture should be familiar to you by now . . . [YNP]

PLATE 42. *Bridalveil Fall. Ca.1867.* Mammoth Plate. While this image is attributed to Watkins, the appearance of a small figure perched jauntily on the rock in the foreground is disconcertingly characteristic of Weed's style. Watkins virtually never included a figure in the scene. [YNP]

PLATE 43. Carleton Watkins. *Bridalveil Fall. Ca.1867.* Mammoth Plate. [YNP]

PLATE 44. Carleton Watkins. *Nevada Fall. Ca.1867.* Mammoth Plate. [YNP]

PLATE 45. Carleton Watkins. *Three Brothers. 1861.* [YNP]

PLATE 46. Anonymous. *Carleton Watkins being led from his studio by his son Collis, following the San Francisco earthquake on April 18, 1906.* Snapshot. [YNP]

PLATE 47. Eadweard Muybridge. *Valley of the Yosemite, Early Morning from Moonlight Rock.* Mammoth Plate. [YNP]

PLATE 48. Eadweard Muybridge. *Tenaya Canyon from the Four Mile Trail.* Mammoth Plate. [YNP]

PLATE 49. Eadweard Muybridge. *South Dome. 1872.* Mammoth Plate. South Dome was the early name given Half Dome; it would have been an arduous climb to reach this particular vantage point on the wall of Yosemite opposite the point from which we usually view the Dome. [YNP]

PLATE 50. Eadweard Muybridge. *Edge of Upper Yosemite Falls. 1872.* Mammoth Plate. [YNP]

PLATE 51. Eadweard Muybridge. *Nevada Fall and Liberty Cap from Glacier Point. 1872.* Mammoth Plate. [YNP]

PLATE 52. Eadweard Muybridge. *Self-Portrait on Contemplation Rock, Glacier Point. 1872.* Stereograph. Muybridge is often remembered less for his Yosemite pictures than for his subsequent "Animal Locomotion Series" (this was the series that included the classic action photo proving a galloping horse takes all four feet off the ground at the same time). Well, in a strange way, it turns out that this self-portrait at Glacier Point played a part in making all that following work possible. (The story is quite convoluted, and if the account I offer here isn't entirely accurate — well then, it's *better* than accurate!) It seems that while Muybridge was spending the summer of 1872 photographing in the Sierra, his attractive young wife Flora was back in San Francisco having an affair with another man. Learning of this infidelity upon his return, Muybridge arrived at a simple and direct solution to the problem: he shot the man dead on the spot. This was not permissible, however, even in San Francisco, and he was charged with murder. But when the issue came to trial, his lawyer entered a plea of Not Guilty by reason of Insanity, and as *evidence . . .* submitted

this picture! Muybridge's publisher, William Rulofson, testified for the defense that "no sane man would venture" to the brink of a precipice overhanging a Valley 3,400 feet below (and for good measure added he also thought it very strange that Muybridge would sometimes refuse to take a picture, no matter how much money was offered him to do it, simply because it did not suit his artistic taste — or to put it another way, that being an artist *per se* was evidence of insanity). Muybridge was acquitted. [P]

PLATE 53. Carleton Watkins. *Vernal Fall. Ca.1867.* [YNP]

PLATE 54. Eadweard Muybridge. *Vernal Fall. 1872.* Mammoth Plate. [YNP]

PLATE 55. C.L. Pond. *The Photographers' Camp at Glacier Point. 1872.* Stereograph. A self-portrait. [P]

PLATE 56. C.L. Pond. *Cloud's Rest. 1872.* Stereograph. [P]

PLATE 57. Reilly & Ormsby. *LaMons Cabin, Yosemite Valley* [P]

PLATE 58. Charles Bierstadt. *Vernal Fall. Ca.1872.* Stereograph [P]

PLATE 59. J.J. Reilly & Co. *El Capitan. Ca.1875.* Stereograph. [P]

PLATE 60. Charles Bierstadt. *Mirror View of North & South Dome, Yo Semite Valley Cal. Ca.1872.* [P]

PLATE 61. Gustav Fagersteen. *Yosemite or Bust. 1877.* Stereograph. A self-portrait, with Fagersteen standing beside his darkroom wagon; another view of the wagon reveals the words "Gustav Fagersteen, Artist" painted in florid script across the back. [P]

PLATE 62. Gustav Fagersteen. *Group Portrait, Hunting Party. Ca.1880.* By mid-summer, Yosemite Fall often dwindle to a mere trickle, and so here a suitably impressive torrent was *painted in* on the original negative before printing. Art steps in where nature fails, as they say. [YNP]

PLATE 63. Gustav Fagersteen. *Group portrait. Ca.1880. [YNP]*

PLATE 64. Gustav Fagersteen. *Group portrait. Ca.1880.* [YNP]

PLATE 65. Gustav Fagersteen. *Group portrait. Ca.1880.* [YNP]

PLATE 66. Gustav Fagersteen. *Group portrait. Ca.1880.* [YNP]

PLATE 67. George Fiske. *Self-Portrait. Ca.1890.* [YNP]

PLATE 68. George Fiske. *Yosemite Fall in Winter. Ca.1890.* [YNP]

PLATE 69. George Fiske. *The Valley in Summer. Ca.1890.* [YNP]

PLATE 70. George Fiske. *The Valley in Winter. Ca.1890.* [YNP]

PLATE 71. George Fiske. *Inspiration Point, Winter. Ca.1885.* [YNP]

PLATE 72. Anonymous. *Hold-up of the Yosemite Stage. 1905.* Snapshot. [YNP]

PLATE 73. Anonymous. *Mrs. Ralph & Celeste at Glacier Point. 1914.* Photo postcard. [P]

PLATE 74. Anonymous. *At Overhanging Rock, Glacier Point. 1920.* Photo Postcard. It they stand up, he goes down... [P]

PLATE 75. Anonymous. *Best's Studio. Ca.1905.* [P]

PLATE 76. Julius Boysen. *Self-Portrait. 1901.* Boysen appears here on the left, with his brother and father. [YNP]

PLATE 77. Julius Boysen. *Indian Woman and Child. 1902.* [YNP]

PLATE 78. Julius Boysen. *The Fallen Monarch, Mariposa Grove of Big Trees. Ca.1903.* Many variants of this photograph exist, each depicting a different group of tourists; my theory is that Boysen photographed each incoming stage this way, then raced ahead to the Valley to process the pictures for them by the time they figured out how to get the damn stagecoach back off the tree... [YNP]

PLATE 79. Ted Orland. *Self-Portrait Atop Half Dome. 1977.* Viki Lang & Jon Organ were along for the climb, and assisted in the taking of this picture. [P] (Hi Viki! Hi Jon!)

PLATE 80. Taber Studio, San Francisco. *James Hutchings. Ca.1890.* [YNP]

PLATE 81. Julius Boysen. *Switchbacks on the Big Oak Flat Road Leading into Yosemite Valley. 1902.* The written histories of Yosemite

often have a way of ovelooking commonplace events that were central to every visitors' experience; this photograph, by contrast, renders vividly evident the all-pervasive layer of dust which each summer visitor collected. Also, we're accustomed today to marvelling at the lush greenery of the Valley, but Ansel Adams once pointed out to me that all the roads in the Park were unpaved before about 1930, and by mid-summer the foliage for twenty feet to each side of those roads displayed a uniform cement-gray coating of dust. "About Zone VII", he added... [YNP]

PLATE 82. Anonymous. *20 Real Photographs 50¢. Ca.1920.* Reproduced here life-size. [P]

PLATE 83. Ted Orland. *Ansel Adams Photographing in Yosemite Valley. 1975.* [P]

Additional Sources

✦✦✦

In any field there are but a handful of books that truly capture the essence of their subject. Some from that handful appear concerned with only a small facet of the subject, but do so in such graceful and irresistable manner as to lead us inextricably to larger truths, while others encompass topics broad and seemingly removed from the issue at hand, yielding the meta-pattern from which the particulars of our reality are cut. This short bibliography, being both selective and eclectic, concerns itself only with such rare pieces — work which is both engaging on its own account as literature, and which provides us with the basis for a richer understanding of our relationship with Yosemite.

The Yosemite Book. By Josiah Whitney, State Geologist for the Geological Survey of California. Published 1868, in an edition of 250 copies; an excessively rare book. Whitney's writing is to literature as dry granola is to taste — functional, but hardly inspiring. Redeeming that shortcoming, however, are the books marvelous illustrations, which take the form of two large fold-out maps (one of Yosemite Valley, and the other of the surrounding portion of the Sierra Nevada Range) and twenty-eight original photographic prints (twenty-four by C.E. Watkins, and four by W. Harris). The size of the edition of *The Yosemite Book* was determined by the stamina of the photographer — in this case the limit being reached upon printing 250 of each of those 28 images that were to be mounted onto blank book pages. A year following the publication of the volume, it was reprinted in much smaller format and much greater numbers — *sans* photographs — under the title *The Yosemite Guide-Book*.

Discovery of the Yosemite. By Lafayette Bunnell, M.D. Published in 1880, with four editions running through 1911; recently reissued in paperback. Bunnell had no formal training in either writing or medicine, but did creditable service in both areas, serving as surgeon for the "Mariposa Batallion", and later setting down his recollections of "the discovery of the Yosemite, and the Indian War of 1851 that led to that event". Whatever his account lacks in literary finesse is more than compensated for by its earnestness and attention to detail, including quotes from all the principals involved in this American morality play. Along the way, the book also provides a fascinating (albeit unintentional) overview of the utter inexplicability of the Indian culture as it appeared to Western eyes.

The Mountains of California. By John Muir. First published in 1894, enlarged in 1911, and currently available in paperback. It is not without reason that Muir's writings remain popular to this day: he combines a Classicist's appreciation for the underlying structure of Nature with a Romantic's responsiveness to the emotional quality of its visible forms. Moreover, he unites these two modes of thinking in a manner that bridges the philosophical distance between nineteenth century Transcendentalism and twentieth century ecological concerns.

All Muir's writings are autobiographical, but perhaps more so here than in his book *The Yosemite*. While *The Mountains of California* contains only brief references to Yosemite Valley *per se*, the writing is singularly warm and personal, recounting the large and small discoveries that taken together reveal the depth and range of Muir's vision.

In The Heart of The Sierras. By James Hutchings. Published in 1886; a rare book. Despite the book's sheer length, Hutchings renders the nineteenth century readers' penchant for endless detail palatable through his flair for presenting information as entertainment. (With 496 pages, 128 line cuts, 24 photo-lithographs, 29 chapters and 347 sub-heads, try to think of it as a Victorian *Time* magazine). A multitude of topics are covered, including Bunnell's account of the discovery of Yosemite Valley and Whitney's theory of its formation, along with descriptions of all manner of flora and fauna and trails and scenery to be found there. The illustrations — most of them drawn from the author's earlier publication, *Hutchings' California Magazine* — range in quality from indifferent pen-and-ink sketches to expert line engravings to superb photo-lithographs. The copyright to *In The Heart of The Sierras* has long since expired, and I keep hoping that some entrepreneur will opt to reissue this wonderful volume.

A Journal of Ramblings Through the High Sierra of California. By Joseph LeConte. Published in three small editions dated 1875, 1900, and 1930; more recently reissued in paperback. Perhaps each of us can look back and recognize some brief period in our life that was unflawed and sublime, a high point to be savored for its richness and meaning as time passes. The summer of 1870 must surely have been such a time for Joseph LeConte; having arrived at the newly established University of California in 1869 as Professor of Geology and Natural History, he was invited by several of his students at the close of the term to join them for a camping trip in the Sierras. "The trip", he wrote, "was almost an era in my life. We were gone six weeks and visited the Yosemite, the High Sierra, Mono Lake and the volcanoes in the vicinity...We had no tent, but slept under trees with only the sky above us. I never enjoyed anything so much in my life — perfect health, the merry party of young men, the glorious scenery, and, above all, the magnificent opportunity

PLATE 80. Taber Studio, San Francisco. *James Hutchings. Ca.1890.*

for studying mountain origin and structure". Free from the dogmatism that leaves Whitney's writings so pompous, and from the Victorian sentimentality that leaves Hutchings' so affected, LeConte's *Journal* conveys the excitement and exhiliration that result from engaging both mind and senses on a voyage of discovery.

Fiske The Cloudchaser. By Thomas Curran. Published in an edition of one thousand by the Oakland Museum in 1981. Every now and then, amidst the profusion of coffee-table extravaganzas that come down the literary pike, there will appear a small and unexpected gem to reaffirm your faith that true quality is not yet dead. *Fiske The Cloudchaser* is such an offering. It presents, with an elegance born of simplicity, twelve unbound laser-scan reproductions of Fiske photographs (printed in ink tones matching the originals), and a brief but eloquent essay by curator Thomas Curran exploring the larger implications of Fiske's work as it relates to nineteenth century American attitudes toward the landscape.

West of Eden: The Art and Literature of Yosemite. By David Robertson. Published in 1984, and currently available in paperback. Here, at long last, is a book that chronicles the full range of artistic output — in all media — that Yosemite has inspired. David Robertson is by profession a scholar (a Professor of English at University of California at Davis, to be exact) and by avocation a photographer and backpacker. These proved valuable traits for sustaining his love and enthusiasm for Yosemite in the face of endless weeks of often drudgerous library research. The resulting book, though mechanically flawed by mediocre printing, nonetheless testifies to the rapport he shares with the artists he writes about, and is in its own way as valid an artistic effort as theirs.

The Incomparable Valley: A Geologic Interpretation of the Yosemite. By Francois Matthes; edited by Fritiof Fryxell. Available in paperback. It remains a source of astonishment to me that with little more than careful observation and deductive reasoning, one can confidently explain what happened a million years ago a mile beneath the surface of a mountain range that no longer exists! Yet that is exactly what Francois Matthes accomplished in this wonderful collection of essays, each sparkling with insight and love for the subject — as enjoyable for general reading as any good novel, and a lot more informative. Given their beauty and clarity, it is saddening that his writings achieved wide recognition only after his death, having been limited to publication in various government periodicals during his half-century of service for the U.S. Geological Survey.

History of the Sierra Nevada. By Francis Farquhar. First published in 1965, and presently available in paperback. At the time Farquhar undertook to write this history, the source material available consisted of a handful of contemporary accounts of early events, and a dusty mountain of records documenting more recent developments. From this unwieldy stack of raw material, Farquhar fashioned a beautifully balanced and enjoyable text — one that is not only meticulously researched, but also spiked with observations and anecdotes drawn from his own extensive backpacking experiences in the Sierra. Though the chapters on current events are now dated, *History of the Sierra Nevada* remains the definitive overview of its subject, just as his earlier *Yosemite, Big Trees, and the High Sierra: A Selective Bibliography* (Univ. of California Press, 1948; now a rare book) remains the best source for tracing the early writings generated by the exploration and development of the area.

PLATE 81. Julius Boysen. *Switchbacks on the Big Oak Flat Road Leading into Yosemite Valley. 1902.*

Looking at Photographs. By John Szarkowski, Director of the Department of Photography at the Museum of Modern Art, New York. Published in 1973, and widely available in paperback. If you are not yourself a photographer, but have more than a passing interest in knowing what makes a photograph work, you should have this book. The structure of the book is quite straightforward — the author has selected one image from the work of each of one hundred photographers represented in the Collection at MOMA, and has written about that image in terms of the interests of the photographer, the technical and social constraints of the period, and the conceptual premises that led to its creation. Szarkowski has a wonderful way with words, imparting insight and information with clarity and humor; as he writes in the preface, "...as a rule, photography has not developed in a disciplined and linear manner, but has rather grown like an untended garden, making full use of the principles of random selection, laissez-faire, participatory democracy, and ignorance."

PLATE 82.

Backcountry Journal: Reminiscences of a Wilderness Photographer. By Dave Bohn. Published in a small edition in 1974; a rare book. Dave Bohn numbers among the most important and — in keeping with his own inclinations — one of the least visible artists working today. Of the several books he has authored, the most remarkable may prove to be the small collection of essays brought together in *Backcountry Journal: Reminiscences of a Wilderness Photographer.* The subtitle could not be more apt: while most present-day landscape photographers rarely tote their gadget bags more than twenty feet from a scenic turnout, Dave Bohn has packed his equipment to K2 in the Himalaya, to Katmai Wilderness in Alaska. In this book, however, photographs play a secondary role — what is primary are the writings, his first-person sharing of the insights that come from personally *experiencing* the land, and from the process of slowly re-investing that insight into his photographs. Bohn's *Journal* ranks with Weston's *Daybooks* in revealing for us not simply what a photograph is *of*, but also what it is *about*...

Era of Exploration: The Rise of Landscape Photography in the American West, 1860-1885. By Weston Naef, in collaboration with James Wood. Published in 1975. It is a delight for the reader when a book such as *Era of Exploration* arrives to lay out for us the large questions and fundamental premises upon which a whole field of study rests. In broadest terms, the authors here ask, "Why photograph landscapes? What did the landscape *mean* to the nineteenth century viewer? What were the influences acting upon the important photographers of that era?" The text is eminently readable and the illustrations beautifully reproduced; if the book has flaws, they are the best kind — the inevitable mistakes that can arise from having courage to offer conclusions based upon a still-unfolding body of data. And indeed the small-minded who mistake facts for ideas have circled hungrily around this volume, nibbling away at a date here, disputing an attribution there, and generally demanding that *their* footnote make it into the next edition. As Nasrudin said long ago, "The dogs always bark as the caravan passes..."

Ansel Adams: Yosemite and the Range of Light. Published in 1979, and currently available both in hardcover and in a smaller-format softcover edition. Ansel Adams attempted a wide range of subject matter during his 60-year career, but it is almost certainly his landscapes — and particularly those of Yosemite and the High Sierra — that will endure most powerfully. That being the case, this book, with its 116 superbly reproduced laser-scan illustrations, may well represent the definitive edition of is most important work.

In comparing Adams' Yosemite photographs with those by Watkins or Muybridge, it is striking that while there are obvious technical differences, the artistic *premises* underlying their efforts were amazingly similar. Indeed, many critics have concluded — without attaching any negative connotation to the judgement — that Adams was in essence a nineteenth century artist, depicting a benign landscape untouched by tourists, automobiles, pollution, electric wires, or social change.

But while the content of Adams' work approximated that of his nineteenth century counterparts, his style and technique were vastly more sophisticated. Perhaps as a result of his early musical training, Adams frequently described his approach to photography in musicians' terms, and indeed the images themselves seem to validate that interpretation. In a photograph like *Clearing Winter Storm, Yosemite* (which serves as the cover illustration for *Yosemite and the Range of Light*), he sets up a temporal counterpoint in which a fleeting passage of light and cloud is modulated against the geologic permanence of primeval cliffs. He likewise sets up a tonal counterpoint of light and dark, waiting for a shaft of sunlight to illuminate Bridalveil Fall at the very moment a darkening cloud envelops El Capitan; and finally he sets up a spatial counterpoint of near against far,

allowing the viewer to absorb the detail from large trees in the foreground and then subconsciously project that same texture into the distant forest, thereby creating an illusion of limitless detail and depth.

Yosemite and the Range of Light is only one of a dozen or more books featuring Adams' work; add to that his own Basic Photo Series of technical books, and his annual Yosemite Photography Workshop (which continues now under the auspices of Ansel Adams Gallery), and you have some hint of the tremendous effect Adams has had upon the photographic community and the public at large. So pervasively has his vision become ours that many of the million people each year who photograph Yosemite Valley do so with the hope that, if everything turns out just right, the result will not simply look like Yosemite, it will look like *an Ansel Adams photograph* of Yosemite.

PLATE 83. Ted Orland. *Ansel Adams Photographing in Yosemite Valley. 1975.*